Guess It

Guess It

By The Lynchsters
with Brendan D. Lynch

1776 Press

Printed in the United States of America. For information, email authorlynch@gmail.com, editor@1776press.com, or contact the Aardvark Princess, if you can find her. Try luring her with bacon.

Guess It
Copyright 2017
Written by *The Lynchsters* with Brendan D. Lynch
ISBN 978-0-9825243-4-3

This is a work of fiction from the minds of fifth grade students in Mr. Lynch's class. Incidents and places in our book are all ideas from the minds of students, although real facts were used to create the clues. This is supposed to be a challenging book, so don't be discouraged if you don't get things on the first try. Aardvark Princess will forgive you as long as you feed her bacon. In this book you must read the clue-filled paragraphs and figure out what each paragraph is talking about. To find out if you are correct or not you must flip to the back of the page. There you will find your legendary answer, determining whether you have failed or won the challenge. (Cue heroic music.) Anyway, if you are even reading this page, that's weird, because who reads the copyright page anyway?

Printed in the United States of America

1776 Press Wethersfield, CT

We would like to dedicate this book to Mr. Lynch's 2015-2016 fifth grade class, which was his class the year before we arrived. Their book, *Just Don't Do It: 1,665 Things You Should Never Do* sold enough copies to provide us with the money to publish this book.

We would also like to dedicate this book to his future fifth grade class, so they can write an amazing book like ours. We want to thank Lauren Stekler, a high school student who helped us out, for sacrificing her Tuesday time to help us.

Lastly, we would like to dedicate this book to our wonderful teacher, Mr. Lynch. Thank you for all the support. We couldn't have done this without you.

The Lynchsters

Contributing Authors

Audrey Alexander
Anisha Alpuri
Tyler Asarro-Gracy
Annie Bruder
Sharanya Chatterjee
Daniel Choi
Dante Cirikovic
McKenna Connelly
Grace Deng
Deya Gorodnitskiy
Zoey Hatinen
David Hoffman
Cameron Kimble
Teja Lakamraju
Ryan Lord
Sawyer Morris
Lexi Pancavage
Arin Rakshe
Dylan Schweitzer
Ethan Sloat
Samantha Tacinelli
Berra Tasdan
Owen White

Introduction
By *The Lynchsters*

Welcome to our somewhat crazy book, *Guess It*. This book was written by 23 fifth graders from Avon, CT. That would be us. The process was hard, especially with so many authors. It took us a bit of time to even choose our subject. Even with many writers, it still took months to finish our first draft. Then came the revising and editing. This also took a month or two, since, you know, we're only fifth graders! Finally, we ran an international design contest to choose our cover. We had to vote several times a day on the designs, and give feedback to the designers.

Even though there were challenges, this process was made easier with so many people involved, and of course, our awesome teacher, Mr. Lynch. Anyway, our book is about a noun, verb, or date you have to guess by reading the clues in the paragraphs. There are five categories: Who Am I? What Am I? Where Am I? What Am I Doing? When Am I? We would like to thank Mr. Lynch's previous class for helping fund this project through the sales of *their* book. Reading this will make you smile, laugh, feel puzzled, and hopefully you'll even learn a thing or two.

Mr. Lynch taught us many things, but teaching us how to write a book was one of the coolest. It was an awesome experience! We hope you enjoy our book. So, go buy a hot dog, sit outside and start reading. If it's cold out, wear a jacket. If you're a vegetarian, then buy a veggie dog. Thanks for reading, and enjoy!

A Few Final Thoughts...
By Brendan D. Lynch

Since this was the second time my students wrote and published a book, I figured this experience would be a lot easier. That is just one of the many lies I told myself. My students, in an attempt to replicate the success of *Just Don't Do It: 1,665 Things You Should Never Do*, wanted to go bigger. Literally.

The book you are holding in your hands is twice the size of the book from the year before. Well, what does bigger really mean? It means more time writing, more time editing, more time formatting, and more money needed for each copy. Luckily, all of that worked out, and they pulled it off.

While it is possible to fast-track the writing and editing of a book with so many authors, challenges arise. Writing differs. Grammar differs. Humor differs. It takes a lot of work to mesh everything together – to make it one piece of writing as opposed to a big mishmash.

The first book was mostly funded by a generous grant from the Avon Education Foundation, with the idea that future books could be self funded by book sales. **All** profits from the sales of *both* books go to support future writing projects for students. Besides those profits, this book was funded by some anonymous donations, and from book sales generated through the *LOL Project*, an amazing charity organization started by Ariella Reynolds (a past student) to get copies of *Just Don't Do It: 1,665 Things You Should Never Do* into the hands of sick kids in hospitals throughout the northeast. Enjoy!

Who Am I?

I am a famous female singer. I used to sing country music, but I now sing pop. I have over 10 albums, but only a few of them are pop. I became famous when I released my first song called "Tim McGraw" in 2006. It was a top hit, and I was a famous singer from then on. When I released the song "22," I was 22 years old. Who am I?

When I was eight years old my adventure began. I moved into a professor's house with my two brothers and one sister because we were sent away from our home. It all started when I was playing hide and seek. I hid in an old wardrobe. I moved deeper and deeper into the coats until I ended up in a winter wonderland that contained one single lamppost. Who am I?

I am an orange bear with a red shirt. I have bunch of animal friends. One is a pig! Sometimes I like to sit and eat my favorite food, honey. Yum! I've been in movies before, and on TV. I can be a small or a big stuffed animal. The last part of my name rhymes with *do*. Who am I?

I am a famous abolitionist. I was alive during the Civil War period. In fact, I was one of the Civil War heroes at the time. I escaped to the North, but devoted almost my whole life into helping other slaves escape to the North where they would have freedom. They didn't have to worry about being whipped or anything else painful. I encouraged them to keep going when they were scared. Who am I?

ANSWER: Taylor Swift

ANSWER: Lucy Pevensie - Chronicles of Narnia

ANSWER: Winnie the Pooh

ANSWER: Harriet Tubman

I can run like the wind. My suit is just plain yellow and red. A lightning bolt is what made me a speedster. If not for the speed force, when I run I would create an explosion the same of an atomic bomb. I can go so fast that I can be in any place at the same time. This is called transit-time velocity. Who am I?

I was the leader of the Jedi High Council for a long time. People who see me think they are stronger than me, but is size all that matters to you? I may be small, but I am one with the force. I am also wise as I have lived for more than 800 years. I have trained many young ones. One of my famous quotes is "Do. Or do not. There is no try." Who am I?

I am small and quick. My nemesis has been in a lot of pain because of me. I can make you laugh without speaking. In fact, my nemesis and I both make you laugh while we are silent. He will never capture me. He may come close, but he never will. I may be a cartoon, but I am smarter than I act. Who am I?

My crazed smile will give you nightmares. I am very evil. I once killed a superhero who helped my biggest enemy. I am a criminal mastermind. I may only be a character on a show, but I can still be scary enough to make you afraid in real life. I am the most terrifying clown ever known. Who am I?

ANSWER: The Flash

ANSWER: Yoda

ANSWER: Jerry (From Tom & Jerry)

ANSWER: Joker

I am very famous for my patriotic deeds. I was a patriot for the American Revolution. I was born in the North End of Boston. I used to be a silversmith. Some people say I was America's hero. I am most famous for my midnight ride. Who am I?

I am half human and half robot. I am part of the Teen Titans team. I am in the Justice League, too. I have a red light bulb as one of my eyes. My other eye is just a normal eye like other people. I like to play tag with my best friend, Beast Boy. Who am I?

In 2017, I was tied for the winningest quarterback in the NFL after my Super Bowl win. I was tied with Brett Favre at 186 wins. Tom Brady was right behind me and Brett at 183 wins in 2017. I won two super bowls with two different teams. Both of my teams' mascots were horses. Who am I?

I have crazy hair and I like to wear jumpsuits. I play the guitar and love dancing. I was born in Tupelo, Mississippi and died in Memphis, Tennessee. A lot of people didn't like my dancing, and said it was a disgrace. I loved Rock and Roll. I am often referred to as "The King Of Rock And Roll" for being an inspiration to a lot of people. Who Am I?

ANSWER: Paul Revere

ANSWER: Cyborg

ANSWER: Peyton Manning

ANSWER: Elvis Presley

I like playing tag with my best friend, Cyborg. I like living in the big T house in the middle of the ocean. I work with a team called the Teen Titans. My skin is green. I got my superpower when a martian with shape-shifting powers gave me a blood transfusion. Who am I?

I am on many posters. I am make believe, but supposedly based on a real person. I am, in my opinion, "a great uncle." I encouraged many to join the army. I am one of the mascots of America. Who am I?

I am one of the best football players of all time. I played in the league from the 1980's to the 2000's. I played the game for two decades and had so many great years. I held almost all the records for my position by the time I retired in 2002. My position is wide receiver. I won three super bowls as a football player. Who am I?

I play soccer and my position is forward. I was the youngest person on the U.S national soccer team in 2009. I wrote a book series called *The Kicks*, which is based on soccer, but is realistic fiction. I won the Olympic gold and the FIFA Women's World Cup. I also won the U.S Soccer Federation female athlete of the year award. My soccer number #13. Who am I?

ANSWER: Beast Boy

ANSWER: Uncle Sam

ANSWER: Jerry Rice

ANSWER: Alex Morgan

I was in over 10 shows or movies. I have two siblings, an older sibling, and a younger sibling. I play a main role in Jessie and Bunk'd. I started acting at age four. My last name is something that you might have when you go shopping. Who am I?

I am an American hero who is known for spying and serving in the American Revolution. I went to college at age 14 at Yale in New Haven, Connecticut. After I went to college I became a school teacher. I spied for George Washington and the Continental Army. My last words were "I only regret that I have but one life to give for my country." Who am I?

Some people consider me one of the biggest winners in football history. I live up to that with four Super Bowl appearances and four wins. I was the first player ever to win three Super Bowl MVPs. I played for the 49ers and the Chiefs. I played Quarterback and was one of the best. One of my greatest achievements is never throwing an interception in any Super Bowl. Who am I?

I was a baseball player, but I retired. My team won 27 world series, which is the most in the MLB. I helped my team win five World Series. I played left field, and my batting average was .310. I had 1,311 RBIs in my career. I am referred to as Mr. November. I retired in 2014. Who am I?

ANSWER: Peyton List

ANSWER: Nathan Hale

ANSWER: Joe Montana

ANSWER: Derek Jeter

When I was president, I wanted to end slavery because I thought that it was unfair. Some people called me Honest. I was very tall at six feet four inches. I also wore a tall black hat, which made me look even taller. I was the 16th president of the United States of America. I did not finish my term in office because something bad happened to me. Who am I?

I am extremely strong. I'm also in comics and have several movies about me. I can fly. I don't like Batman. You could say I hate him. My name starts with an S. I have a fortress and I cannot be around kryptonite or I will get very weak. Who Am I?

I am kind of a big deal around the U.S. I was born in 1946. I have been one of the wealthiest men in the U.S. for a long time. My first wife's name was Ivana. I have to deal with a lot of issues everyday. Once elected, I became the 45th person to hold a very powerful position. Who am I?

I was a famous African American female poet. I was born in Senegal/Gambia. I was a slave and was kidnapped when I was only eight years old. I lived for 31 years. I wrote 41 poems and eight books. I was around during the time of the American Revolution. Who am I?

ANSWER: Abraham Lincoln

ANSWER: Superman

ANSWER: Donald Trump

ANSWER: Phyllis Wheatley

I am famous for my well known book series. Many kids like to read my books for fun or to see crazy and strange records. I was an American cartoonist and entrepreneur. Believe it or not, I never finished high school. I was the New York City handball champion. I wrote a book about it, too. Who am I?

My famous quote is "I tawt I taw a puddy tat." I am a male yellow canary. I go by three names. My cartoon debut was in 1942. I am a fictional character on Looney Tunes. My creators were Friz Freleng and Bob Clampett. Who am I?

I am defined as a humanly physical perfection. I took Super Soldier Serum, which made me a superhuman. I am a hero. In fact, some people call me a symbolic U.S. hero. My sidearm or my protection is what a lot of people know me for. I am one of the most loved superheroes in Marvel Comics. Who am I?

I was alive during the Revolutionary War period. I am famous for writing a letter called "Remember the Ladies." I wrote over 3,000 letters in my lifetime. I never went to school, but I was well educated. I died of typhoid fever. Who am I?

ANSWER: Robert Ripley

ANSWER: Tweety Pie/ Tweety bird/ Tweety

ANSWER: Captain America

ANSWER: Abigail Adams

I live in Forest Hill, New York. My parents died in a plane crash, so I went to go live with my aunt and uncle. My aunt and uncle's names are Ben and May Parker. I got my powers at a high school after a spider bit me. I have superhuman strength and one more cool superpower. Who am I?

Some people believe in me and some people don't. I am known by two names. I live in a very cold place. I love children, and they love me. I celebrate at a certain day every year. I am usually depicted as wearing red, and bringing presents to people. Who am I?

I am not very well known, but I am an important military figure. I was in charge of many soldiers. I fought in the French and Indian war alongside George Washington. I was the royally appointed governor in Massachusetts. I was commander of all British forces in North America. Who am I?

I am a hero to many. I am nicknamed the Flea because I am short and fast, as well as for my wicked soccer skills. I was crowned the World's best soccer player more than once. I'm very well known. I joined the team when I was 13. Who am I?

ANSWER: Spider Man

ANSWER: Santa Clause

ANSWER: Thomas Gage

ANSWER: Lionel Messi

I was the first president and founding father of United States. You can find my picture on the one dollar bill. There is city and state named after me. I was part of the American Revolution. There are many paintings that picture me. One is while crossing the Delaware river. My face is carved on Mount Rushmore. Who am I?

I'll tell you a little bit about myself. I invented a lot of things including bifocals, the lightning rod, and much, much, more. I was a newspaper printer and editor. I was a founding father of the United States. I was one of the signers of the Declaration of Independence. Who am I?

I am a singer and songwriter. In high school I liked to act and sing a lot. I have a lot of hit albums like "Born This Way," "Just Dance," "Poker Face," and a lot more. I was the 2017 Super Bowl Halftime Performer. I have sang with Paul Mccartney I have also sang with Elton John at the "Grammy's" once. I have six Grammys for my music. Who am I?

I set the record for the most saves in an Olympic soccer game in 2014. I play for the Colorado Rapids. I have a biography dedicated to me. People call me the Gallant of Defeat. I have Tourette Syndrome. That syndrome actually helped me be the elite goalkeeper that I am. I wasn't really that good when I started but I became a very elite goalie. Who am I?

ANSWER: George Washington.

ANSWER: Benjamin Franklin

ANSWER: Lady Gaga

ANSWER: Tim Howard

I played for the University of North Carolina when I was in college. I got my nicknames because of my dunks. Most people know me for playing on different team, but I also played for the Washington Wizards in the NBA in the 2000s. A lot of people use my number in basketball to be like me. Nike makes clothing dedicated to me. I am a retired legend. Who am I?

I coach a sport. I live in Massachusetts. I coach one of the best teams in the NFL. Before I joined this team, I coached the Browns and the Jets. I won seven Super Bowl championships. Who Am I?

I was born in Milan, Ohio. I had six siblings. Also, my wife and I had six kids - three daughters and three sons. My father was an exiled political activist from Canada. I am a famous inventor. I invented something that most people use every day that provides light. My middle name is Alva. Who am I?

I am a retired soccer legend. I am widely regarded as the best soccer player ever alive. I was once the best-paid soccer player in the world. I played for my country's national team when I was only 16. I played professional soccer starting at 15. I scored 77 goals in 91 soccer games with my country's national team. I won three FIFA World Cups. November 19th is dedicated to me when I scored my 1000th goal in all competitions. Who am I?

ANSWER: Michael Jordan

ANSWER: Bill Belichick

ANSWER: Thomas Edison

ANSWER: Pelé

I am a very well known inventor. I am also a technological entrepreneur. I am the co-founder of one of the largest companies in the world. My company is now the owner of many devices that people all over the world use everyday. I produced many technological advances. Who am I?

I am a famous person. I was born on August 5, 1930 and died on August 25, 2012. I was a space engineer, but after that I made history. My name starts with an N and ends with a L. I had a very famous quote while standing on a rock. I was the first man to go up and walk on the moon. Who am I?

I was a leader in the Civil-Rights movement. The name my parents gave me was Michael, but people know mw by a different name. I was a peaceful protester and was non-violent. My father also had the same name as me. One of my famous speeches is remembered to this day. I also have a day named after me. Who am I?

I was a professional baseball player for the New York Yankees. My batting average was .342 and I had 2,214 RBIs in my whole career. I also played for the Red Sox, but I am most famous for playing for the New York Yankees. I was a pitcher and an outfielder. I played baseball for 22 seasons. Who am I?

ANSWER: Steve Jobs

ANSWER: Neil Armstrong

ANSWER: Martin Luther King Jr.

ANSWER: Babe Ruth

In 1950, I founded the missionaries of charity. They have a vow, "to give wholehearted free service to the poorest of the poor." They have over 4,500 sisters and were present in 133 countries as of 2012. In 1962, I was awarded the Ramon Magsaysay peace prize. Also, in 1979, I received the Nobel Peace Prize. I was known in the Catholic Church as Saint _____ of Calcutta. I also spoke five languages. They were Bengali, Albanian, Serbian, English, and Hindi. Who am I?

I am a famous person on television. People think I am mean to people. I have a British accent. I'm a judge for a show with the abbreviation AGT. I was born in London, England. I was one of the judges on an American singing show, an American talent show, and a British talent show. Who Am I?

I was a civil rights leader and I strongly believed in peace and I was against war. I made a change that made my home country free from British rule. I walked an exhausting walk of 388 kilometers with many followers. I walked from Ahmedabad to Dandi. This was called the Salt Satyagraha. Who am I?

I was a scientist and a vegetarian. I am famous for helping chimpanzees of Tanzania, and for my work with chimps in Gombe. I learned so many things, like what tools that chimpanzees can make. I studied the chimpanzees so much, that I lived with them in the rainforest for 50 years! Who am I?

ANSWER: Mother Teresa

ANSWER: Simon Cowell

ANSWER: Mahatma Gandhi

ANSWER: Jane Goodall

I played for over five teams in my career. My position was midfield. I had a knack for bending my shots on a free kick, crossing, and a long range in passing. I was runner up for being the FIFA World Player of the Year twice. I was inducted into the English Football Hall of Fame in 2008. The team I started my career with was Manchester United. My middle name is Robert Joseph. Who am I?

I was born in 1913 in Alabama. I grew up having to deal with segregation. Almost everywhere I went I was discriminated against. My mother taught me to read. I was great friends with Martin Luther King Jr. I was involved in the March on Washington. I am most famous for not giving up my bus seat to another person. I was fined and put in jail for it, but I helped America become desegregated. Who am I?

I came here to America from Spain, where my father and I made maps. People in my time thought that at the end of the maps you would fall off the edge of the world. I tried getting a better trading route to India, and today I am known by many as a great explorer who helped Europeans learn about the Americas. Who am I?

I was born in 1809 in Britain. I was an English naturalist who was in the Victorian society. I am famous for discovering the line of evolution. I spent three and a half years sailing on the S.S. Beagle. I said, "In the struggle for survival, the fittest win out at the expense of their rivals because they succeed in adapting themselves best to the environment." Who am I?

ANSWER: David Beckham

ANSWER: Rosa Parks

ANSWER: Christopher Columbus

ANSWER: Charles Darwin

I was widely regarded as one of the most significant and celebrated sports figures of the 20th century. I lived in Scottsdale, Arizona. I died because of Septic shock on June 3, 2016. I was an American professional boxer and activist. I had seven daughters. Who am I?

I am a Canadian actor, and I started doing comedy for my friends when I was in elementary school. I was Horton's voice in "Horton Hears a Who." I have been in a lot of movies like "How the Grinch Stole Christmas." I have also been in all the "Dumb and Dumber "movies. Who am I ?

I am very a very famous person. I had eight siblings growing up. I had three children, two boys and a girl. I went to Harvard University. I was the 35th president of the United States, which makes me, if I do say so myself, a pretty accomplished person. Unfortunately, I did not get a chance to finish my presidency. Who am I?

I am an American Motion Picture and Television Producer. I'm famous as a pioneer of cartoon films and as the creator of Disneyland. I created a lot of cartoon characters. My favorite one was Mickey Mouse. I won 22 academy awards in my lifetime. I once said, "All our dreams can come true, if we have the courage to pursue them. If you can dream it, you can do it. It's kind of fun to do the impossible." Who am I?

ANSWER: Muhammad Ali

ANSWER: Jim Carrey

ANSWER: John F. Kennedy

ANSWER: Walt Disney

I was president for most of World War II. I was the President for the beginning of the war and left office a month before it ended. I have a wife named Eleanor and my children's names are Anna, James, Elliott, Franklin and John. Many people said I could have been the "king of the world." I got my education at Harvard University and Columbia Law School. I am the 32nd President of the United States of America. My Vice President was John Nance Garner. Who Am I?

I was born in 1926. I was adopted when I was nine. I was divorced twice. I was an American actress and a very famous model. Many people know me because I was on TV a lot. I was in 28 movies, two shows, and have written 32 songs. Who am I?

I was born on March 25, 1964. I have one sibling named Curt. I am a writer, I have written at least nine books (though I helped with even more). Out of the nine books I wrote I earned four awards. One of my quotes is "Reading should not be presented to children as a chore, a duty. It should be offered as a gift." My passion is writing fiction. One of my most famous books is *Because of Winn-Dixie*. Who am I?

I am a pretty well-known famous actress. When I was younger, I had a passion for dance, ballet. At the age of 22 I starred in the film *Roman Holiday*. I am mostly known for my movie based on me, *Breakfast at Tiffany's*. I was in 29 movies in my lifetime. I won two Oscars. Who am I?

ANSWER: Franklin D. Roosevelt

ANSWER: Marilyn Monroe

ANSWER: Kate Dicamillo

ANSWER: Audrey Hepburn

I am an icon for a certain restaurant. I am a southerner. I love a certain kind of fried meat. I was a celebrity in the food industry. I died, but I still appear in ads. My first name makes me sound like I'm in the military, but I'm not. My catchphrase is: It's finger-lickin' good! Who am I?

I am a fictional character. I am the star of many books and many movies. I have a magic wand. Some people say I am a wizard. I was educated at Hogwarts School of Witchcraft and Wizardry. I was picked into Gryffindor. My creator is J. K. Rowling. Who am I?

I was born in the province of Massachusetts Bay, in 1711. I went to Harvard University at age 12, and graduated at age 16. I played a famous role in the Boston Massacre. At the time I was Royal Governor of Massachusetts. I was 4th of 12 children. My father, who was a wealthy merchant, had the same name as me. Who am I?

I am a mythical creature that some people think is real. I am a woman that has magical powers. I usually wear a black cloak, and a pointy hat. I love to fly on a broomstick, and I hate kids. I think they are ugly, annoying, and disgusting little rats. Who Am I?

ANSWER: Colonel Sanders

ANSWER: Harry Potter

ANSWER: Thomas Hutchinson

ANSWER: A Witch

I was born in Alabama in 1913. When I was a senior in high school, I set three high school world records in track & field. I am most famous for being a four time Olympic gold medalist in the 1936 Berlin Olympics. I set three world records and tied one on that day in less than an hour. Who am I?

I was the 33rd president of the U.S. I was a vice president for 82 days. I was born in Missouri on May 8, 1884. I ended a war a few months after I was sworn in. I am the only president to ever drop atomic bombs on two cities. Who am I?

I am one of the most iconic people in the music industry. I was born in Bonn, Germany and I died in Vienna, Austria. I made nine symphonies and 32 piano sonatas, which is a piece of music for only one instrument. I am widely considered the greatest composer ever. Who am I?

I have been the best at my solo sport more than five times. I once held it for 186 weeks, or about 3 years. I was born September 26, 1981. I am 5 feet 9 inches tall. I became a professional when I was only 14 years old! My middle name is Jameka. I was endorsed with Nike in 2013, with Nike tennis shoes dedicated just to me. Who am I?

ANSWER: Jesse Owens

ANSWER: Harry S. Truman

ANSWER: Ludwig Van Beethoven

ANSWER: Serena Williams

I am a fictional comic book character, and I have aired in two movies as of May 2017. I was created by Stan Lee, Dick Ayers, and Jack Kirby. My first appearance was in *Tales to Astonish*. Some people say that I'm a plant. I only say one sentence, which includes me saying my name. Who am I?

I go "quack quack" all the time! I am a duck, but who am I really? I am a cartoon character, and I was played by Tony Anselmo and Clarence Nash. I am in love with Daisy, a VERY pretty duck. Something embarrassing about me is that I only wear a shirt and a sailor's hat.

I am a golfer who won the 2017 Masters. I never got the green jacket until I won the championship. My opponent was Justin Rose, and I almost lost because of some bogies. I've participated in 74 major championships. I made a magical second shot to tie up with Justin Rose. On the last hole, Rose missed a shot, and the door to victory was open. I took the shot, and the ball almost missed the hole, but went in! Who am I?

I am one of the greatest players who ever played in my position. I play for the National Football League (NFL). I won many Super Bowls. My birthday is August 3, 1977. My number is 12. I am married to a famous model. The position I play is has the initials QB. Who am I?

ANSWER: Groot/Baby Groot

ANSWER: Donald Duck

ANSWER: Sergio Garcia

ANSWER: Tom Brady

In Ancient Greek my name means "Glory of Hera." The Romans named me something slightly different. My Roman name is more commonly known than my Greek one. According to legend, after I died I was changed to a god by the gods on Mount Olympus. I defeated many monsters including the Nemean Lion and the astrologian birds as part of my ten labors for High King Eurystheus. Who am I?

I am extremely jolly and tiny. I love to wear Christmas colors. I have very tiny and pointy ears. I love to help make toys. I make sure that the reindeers are doing just right. I guard my home. I have curly and pointy shoes and I love to wear bells. Who am I?

I am a character from an animated cartoon show that was produced in 1989. I wear pearls around my neck. I am yellow. I'm a middle child. I became a vegetarian in season 7. I have been voiced by Yeardley Smith since 1987. I am eight years old and have been that age throughout the sho. I am a talented saxophone player. I live in 742 Evergreen Terrace, Springfield. Who am I?

There are a lot of different variations of picture books about me. It depends on how you make me, but most of the time I am brown. I was alive because of a baker. The people tried to catch me, but I was too smart and quick for them until one animal did actually catch me, as some stories say. I ran away from them because they wanted to eat me. Who am I?

ANSWER: Hercules/ Heracles

ANSWER: Elf of Santa

ANSWER: Lisa Simpson

ANSWER: The Gingerbread man

I am usually considered as a top 10 player in my sport's history. When I grew up, I moved in with my coach because my mom couldn't support me. When I was in high school, I played two sports, football and basketball. I picked the latter. I was named the best player for my sport in Ohio three times in a row. Who am I?

I am a former American competitive swimmer and the most decorated Olympian of all time. If have a total of 28 medals. I also hold the all-time records for Olympic gold medals (23). I won eight gold medals at the 2008 Beijing Games. At the 2012 Summer Olympics in London, I won four gold and two silver medals. At the 2016 Summer Olympics in Rio de Janeiro, I won five gold medals and one silver. This made me the most successful athlete for the Games for the fourth Olympics in a row. Who Am I?

I am the author of an amazingly successful series. It has even been made into a series of movies! Most people know the name of the main character in the series I created. I have a pen name. It is Robert Galbraith. Who am I?

I teach them math, science, writing and more. I also teach them lessons about life. I work in a classroom full of kids. I have to protect kids. Some people like to give me an apple. I have to go through many years of college. Who Am I?

ANSWER: Lebron James

ANSWER: Michael Phelps

ANSWER: Joanne Katherine Rowling (JK Rowling)

ANSWER: Teacher

I was born in 1162 in Mongolia. I married at the very young age of sixteen. I returned to my home in Mongolia after my father died to claim my position as clan chief. I founded the Mongol Empire and I am considered one of the best conquerors ever. I died in 1227 against the Chinese Kingdom. Who am I?

I turned into a professional at my sport when I was only seventeen. A big accomplishment was that at the age of seventeen I won the junior tournament in my sport over Irakli Labadze in singles, and in doubles I won a tournament with Olivier Rochus. I was born in Basel, Switzerland. I once was ranked Top 10 in my sport starting from 2002-2014. I also once was ranked first in my sport for 302 weeks! Who am I?

I am a person who is very motivating. I am a meme that will never die. I help multiple charities. I have been in multiple movies. I have my own merchandise. I have a reality television show. I have a famous clip of me wrestling. It starts off saying, "Watch out, watch out!" Who am I?

I was born in Pisa, Italy on February 15, 1564. I was an astronomer, mathematician, philosopher, engineer, and physicist. I improved the telescope, which helped me study the planets. I earned many friends this way. I am very famous for discovering that the Earth revolves around the Sun. My name in Italian means "from Galilee." Who am I?

ANSWER: Genghis Khan

ANSWER: Roger Federer

ANSWER: John Cena

ANSWER: Galileo

I've been in more than seven movies so far. I am a fictional superhero. More than ten people have played me in all of the movies and shows I've been in. People may say that I'm a bat. I have a sidekick named Robin, but his real name is Tim. I wear black, yellow and a cape. Who I am?

I am a nice guy. I am also the mascot of famous company. I'm really famous. You definitely know me. You can call me an "actor" because I played in Fantasia, Steamboat Willie, Runaway Brain and a bunch more awesome movies. My first cartoon that I was in was "Plane Crazy." Who am I?

Many people know that I tried to save a life. Others thought I would destroy it. I wanted to protect the little boy, and he was so unlucky to have fallen in. I got shot, and people were outraged. Many people would have protests just for me. I will always be remembered as a major animal rights figure. There have been multiple interviews with my killer. Who am I?

I stood straight with a Jamaican flag draped around me. My Puma running shoes had made marks on the track because of my speed. I walked over to the stopwatch and posed for pictures. "My last Olympics in the books," I thought as I was awarded my ninth career gold medal. The Rio sign was carved into it onto the solid gold circle. I had finished my perfect triple triple. Who am I?

ANSWER: Batman

ANSWER: Mickey Mouse

ANSWER: Harambe

ANSWER: Usain Bo

What Am I Doing?

I stood on the line of scrimmage, ready to sprint down the field. I was trying to get open. I looked up and saw defenders scatter around the field. So, I cut through the defenders and got open. Then a kid threw the ball to me and I caught it on my run. Then, I sprinted as fast as I could. I beat the defender and ran straight forward. What am I doing?

My face got slightly pink. I felt like I did the worst thing in my life. I kept asking myself why I did this. It didn't make sense to me anymore. I happened to be the one who just did it. I was so dumb to do this. Saying the complete opposite of what I actually did. What am I doing?

As I looked from the window, I saw what most have never seen. It was glorious, but it looked so rough and rugged. As I got closer, I left out the hatch and got ready to get out. I was very thrilled. As the ship landed, I hit the open hatch button and my excitement filled the sky. As I took my first leap, I felt nothing. It was such a mind-blower. What am I doing?

My teacher went over the packet telling us what to do on each question. The moment my teacher said, "You may began" I took a deep breath. Then I started to do the problems. When I finished I checked over my answers. I did all of the problems again to make sure they were all right. What am I doing?

ANSWER: Playing Football

ANSWER: Lying

ANSWER: Landing on the Moon

ANSWER: Taking a Test

Spreading the frosting was delightful. It felt so satisfying sliding the spoon around and on top of the giant piece of yellowish, spongy goodness. Later, when I finished, I squinted to see in the thick, hot glass. I saw the fluff rising higher and higher, until it was plain gold. I put on my mittens and took it out to cool. When I finished, I made sure that the creamy topping was thick enough to spread. What am I doing?

It felt almost as if I were flying, with the waves passing by me. I flew my arms forward and back, sliding on top of the cool liquid, my feet kicking and dragging at the same time behind my body. As I was breathing in some moments, and holding my breathe in other moments, I was almost touching the wall on the other side. Then I took a deep breath, brought my hands to my hip and chin to my chest, and I flung my legs forward and turned. What am I doing?

My heart pounds. My muscles strain. I can see it. I move towards it, slowly, achingly painfully. Others with the same goal zoom past me with blinding speed. They had taken a more conservative approach. I was sure that I would never stand again as I lurched towards the final goal. What am I doing?

Once again I had to do it. I got it out of the machine and started sorting. I fold the shirt and pants and put it in a basket to bring upstairs.. Chores, chores, chores. Wish they were never there. What am I doing?

ANSWER: Baking a cake

ANSWER: Swimming

ANSWER: Running a race

ANSWER: Doing the laundry

I start packing my bag. "We need to go!" shouts mom. What I'm doing right now usually occur on weekends. When I go to this place I usually watch a movie or just play. Sometimes I can be at this place for multiple days. This place I am going is definitely going to have snacks. I am going somewhere with a friend. What am I doing?

I was imagining pictures in my head. I was in a good mood. I felt like doing this for hours. I was enjoying the feeling of words flowing through my head. I was looking at hundreds of words on a page. When my mom told me to put it down I whined. What am I doing?

Click, Click, Click. The sound that my device is making is just, Click, Click, Click. I turned off my phone because I was done with my conversation with my friend. Then I heard... DING. It was probably a reminder, but nope, it was my friend again. This time she asked me if I could send her a picture of the math homework. I bet she forgot to bring it home. I did it, and then I said my goodbyes and turned off my phone once again. What am I doing?

The snow flew up, and coated my face with a light fluffy covering. I hit something, and then I lost balance and fell. As I got up, another person comes down the snow covered hill and falls next to me. When I got to the bottom of the hill, I pull into the lift area. What am I doing?

ANSWER: Having a sleepover

ANSWER: Reading a book

ANSWER: Texting

ANSWER: Skiing

The wind rushed through my hair as we went around and around. I still couldn't believe that I was on it. It was unbelievable, insane, and incredible at the same time. The excitement just wouldn't stop. I would do it again and again and no one could stop me. Suddenly, everything blurred as we went down at, what felt like, the speed of light. I was screaming as my hands waved in the air. What am I doing?

I think we will go to Main St. then to State Rd. Oh it's the Sullivans' dog. It's running after a squirrel. I'm sweating a lot. My legs are starting to ache. It's getting dark. I should go home and take nap. What am I doing?

My team and I had practiced for a long time. We were born for this day. We were playing the best team in the league, and it was going to be a nail biter. We started the game losing by eight points. At halftime, we were all so tired. By the fourth quarter, we were down by one. I got the ball. All sorts of things were going through my head, but I shot the ball. I made the buzzer beater. What am I doing?

My conscience was telling me that I was going too fast. I slowed down. I could see everyone staring at me. I was never a great speaker in front of an audience. I was very nervous, but I kept on talking. I told myself that everyone had to do this. When I finished and everyone clapped and cheered. What am I doing?

ANSWER: Riding a Roller Coaster

ANSWER: Jogging or running

ANSWER: Playing Basketball

ANSWER: Giving a Speech

I made a mark with strokes of beautiful colors. It was making me happy. Many famous people started off their career just by doing this. Even though, I was using a particular one, you could use different thing to do me or do it in different ways. I had a thought in my head of what I was going to do. This is the beginning of a masterpiece. What am I doing?

I checked two more times to see if I had everything. I was so excited. This was going to be the most amazing trip ever! I rolled my suitcase downstairs and yelled to my parents. I have been waiting to do this since first grade, and now I finally can. I've never been to where I'm going. What am I doing?

I asked for a volunteer and everyone eagerly raised their hands because they wanted to be picked. I chose someone in the front. I asked them to pick a card in my hands and not to tell me what it was. After the person did, I guessed which one they picked. I got it correct. You can use cards or a special kind of a bird for the thing I am doing. What am I doing?

My friends and I are carrying sodas, lemonades, and ice cream. The ice cream is dripping onto the floor. So, you get in a line and you try and pick a short one. When it becomes your turn, you get in and put the harness over your head. It moves fast up a huge hill. You reach the top and you rush down. Where am I?

ANSWER: Drawing

ANSWER: Packing for a vacation

ANSWER: Doing a magic trick

ANSWER: On a ride at an amusement park

I am walking inside a big building, and the parking lot is filled with cars. It's probably because it's Black Friday. I thought to myself, maybe I'll buy some clothes for myself, and then I'll get some lunch. Then, I'll buy some other things for gifts to give to people. My plan sounded great to me, especially with a huge mob of people roaming around the floors of the building. It's good to have a plan. I'm going to get this done faster than a cheetah will run. Where am I?

I am standing in a corn field. All I can see is flashing red all around me. I quickly pull a paper bag out of my pack. I bite off the top and jam it down the barrel. I pull back a piece of flint with all the strength left in me. I look down the sights and pull the trigger. I hear a crack then I look up and I hit my mark. Then repeated my process as another volley flies over my head. What am I doing?

Sometimes I make kids very mad, and they just can't figure me out. There's many versions of me and even some online. Sometimes kids get in trouble for not having me finished. I am the mastermind of your teacher. There's just not enough school hours so they give me to you to do later. What am I?

Women do this on average between 30 and 64 times a year. Men do this on average between 6 and 17 times per year. Most babies do this when they are first born. You did this when you are sad or hurt. What am I doing?

ANSWER: Shopping at a mall

ANSWER: Firing A Musket

ANSWER: Homework

ANSWER: Crying

I am sweating like crazy now. My face is as red as a tomato. I have just completed my first repetition of ten. Now I really feel the burn in my arms and legs. I feel like I can't hold my body up for longer. This is the exercise I must do to stay in shape. What am I doing?

I am going to a place where they have a lot of food. It's very loud where I am going because when something happens, some people start cheering, and the rest are filled with anger. When I get to this place I will see a small round ball fly through the air. There is a man that is dressed in all black at this place. When I leave, I will feel one of these feelings, mad or happy. What am I doing?

When I jump up and down I feel like I'm going to touch the sky. I am with my friends, and we are having a blast. We try to do flips and we fail, but we are okay because we bounce back up when we fall. What am I doing?

A blast of water hits my back, drenching me in water. My soaking wet shirt is stuck to my skin. Now it's my turn to get revenge. I turned towards my opponent just in time to spray him. That was it, game over for him. What am I doing?

ANSWER: Push-ups

ANSWER: Going to a baseball game

ANSWER: Jumping on a Trampoline

ANSWER: Having a Water Gun fight

I can feel the wind coming toward face as I start to run faster every minute. I want to get the best time in my class when I run the mile, and so I'm practicing for the day. I go fast, but not too fast because I need to pace myself and I would lose all my energy if I didn't. What am I doing?

I'm trying to beat the last level and my high score. My fingers are aching. My eyes are focused, staring straight at the screen. Then, I was caught doing nothing so I was grounded. "No electronics for the week!" What am I doing?

You should do this before you eat to get rid of disgusting germs. If you do this every day, you will be healthy and won't get sick. It is very important, as important as doing your homework. My doctor and parents probably tell me to do this every time I see them. "Don't forget to use the soap!" they say. What am I doing?

I have to get up and get dressed first. Long or short sleeve? I look for a something that is appropriate for the day. Wow, it's winter and I've got shorts in my hand, so I find something else. This probably has taken me a few minutes. What am I doing?

ANSWER: Running

ANSWER: Playing on my Phone

ANSWER: Washing my hands

ANSWER: Picking out my clothes

I am waiting until I get the *thumbs up* to begin. I am hyped and ready. I didn't think that they would turn off the lights. There were walls everywhere with holes that I could snipe through. I saw my first target, then ran to a wall and took aim. BEEP! I hit him dead on, so I ran past him to the next wall. Then POW I was hit. I had to stay still and not use my gun for ten seconds. What am I doing?

I looked up, trying to decide where to go. I was about to heave myself up to the top. Then I put my foot there on it to see if it was stable or not. All of the sudden I hear a CRACK sound, and I almost fell. That was a close call. I hang helplessly while my legs dangle. What am I doing?

I stand on a dock straightening a line, so it's straight and has no wrinkles. I wrapped it around a metal rod and throw the line out. Then I slowly pull the line back in. Then the line straightened. I try pulling it back but it won't budge. I see bubbles rising out of the water. Suddenly, a giant silver shadow burst out of the water. What am I doing?

As I walked on to the stage I could feel the lights shining on me. I glanced at the audience and my mind began to race. Nobody spoke. I figured that it was my line! I had forgotten it. I would have to improvise. As I began to say made up sentence, I remembered the words to my sentence, the real one! Phew. As I exited the stage later, I thought of what a disaster that could have been. What am I doing?

ANSWER: Playing laser tag

ANSWER: Climbing a tree

ANSWER: Fishing

ANSWER: Acting in a Play

As I let go of the tiller, the cold salty breeze ran through my hair. The sun gleamed against the water, making it shimmer. I skimmed my hand across the surface of the water. I slowed to a complete stop, and I looked out at the horizon. I saw a dolphin splashing around in the water. What am I doing?

Some people say that the task ahead of me is impossible, or will take forever. The frosty wind chills my skin as I look at the spot where I will build. A big truck came just yesterday to make a suitable pile. My friend says that it does it by piling the stuff up. I will soon dig into it. As I stick the shovel into the snow I hear a nice crunch. What am I doing?

I walked in normally, but my brain was filling with doubts. I had to trust my instincts. No one noticed me until I was almost there. The employee asked me what I was doing. I made up the most convincing lie the employee probably ever heard. Then I proceeded with my criminal mission. I typed in the code and went in. I got my folder and adjusted the weight by taking out some papers, then switched it out making my partner and I very happy. What am I doing?

Mmmm, I smell the scent of fall apples being candied. I love that smell. It was all the way cooled. I sliced into the warm dessert, and distributed it evenly amongst my friends and family. Biting into the tasty dessert, I could feel my teeth crunching into the crust. What am I doing?

ANSWER: Sailing

ANSWER: Making a snow fort

ANSWER: Stealing a diamond

ANSWER: Eating pie

I sit quietly in a metal stand in a tree waiting for the sound of leaves rustling. I hold tensely to the stock of my weapon. I spin my head in a 360 degree rotation all around. I see nothing but trees. I look up to see a squirrel walk on the dry leaves. After waiting an hour I was about to head home, but I saw a big deer with horns the size of a football on either side. I breathe slowly, and then BOOM! What am I doing?

As I adjusted the mask, I breathed in to suction it onto my face. I sat down to put on the wide black shoes. I took unnatural steps into the water. Soon enough I was deep enough to start. I put the little rubber piece into my mouth and dove in. As I examined the many colorful animals I wondered what other life could be below. What am I doing?

As I sit on a seat I can tell that it's going to be a long trip. On this you can go places that are really far away. It would be silly to go somewhere close. As it takes off we go up in the air. I can see everything from up in the sky, and everything is so small. The view is picturesque. What am I doing?

My eyes are closed and I am trying to think about nothing. I lay down, but I could sit up to do it. I will need to stay warm and toasty. I won't forget about the comfy pillow this time. I sometimes have a dream. Sometimes, I have a nightmare, which then makes me wake up. What am I doing?

ANSWER: Hunting Deer

ANSWER: Snorkeling

ANSWER: Riding on a Plane

ANSWER: Sleeping

And I felt my tongue rub over the ball-like sweet, it is the definition of glory! I love this orange flavoring. I wish I could have another one. I always enjoy sweets and candy. As I thought and thought I noticed a hard paper tasting stick. "NOOOOO!" I screamed. This is the END of my glory. What am I doing?

My face was expanding with pain. My knuckles burned, as if they were on fire. I needed to keep on going, I thought. I slowly got up and looked at him. He was smirking, thinking it was the end. The next thing I thought was I was going to wipe that smirk off his face, literally. Moments later he was curled up on the ground and I had him pinned down. The crowd roared with approval of my victory. What am I doing?

It is so hard to concentrate with the sound blaring so loud! If I try to stop at the wrong time, the people around me would not stop. I stop in a traffic jam. I try to focus my mind and concentrate. Left, forward, right. What am I doing?

ANSWER: Licking a lollipop

ANSWER: Wrestling

ANSWER: Driving a car in traffic

When Am I?

I am a holiday that takes places over several nights. Children love me because of the presents. Adults love me because of the social time with the family. I am usually celebrated in the early winter. Another name for me is the Festival of Lights. When am I?

I am a holiday, although not everyone celebrates me. Some people have parties while others just spend time with family. I fall on a specific day every year. There are a lot of traditions people do on this day. Some people that are French call me Noel. In Spanish I am called Nochebuena. When am I?

I heard guns shooting in the sky and asked myself, why were planes were coming in. It was an invasion. I couldn't believe they would attack a paradise island. I saw a plane crash into a large ship. I could see smoke everywhere and I could hardly breathe. If I lived, I would never forget this battle between the Japanese. When am I?

I'm an important day on the calendar to kids every year. You can prepare heavily or not before my date. People buy so much on my day. The most sold food on my date is something sweet. Kids say a famous line while they walk around a neighborhood. When am I?

ANSWER: Hanukkah (November or December)

ANSWER: Christmas (December 25)

ANSWER: December 7, 1941 (Attack on Pearl Harbor)

ANSWER: Halloween (October 31)

It is the day where you can confess your love to the perfect one. Many people get or give chocolates or roses on this day. Teachers may make a project based on this day. Many people get engaged on this day. The colors this day is known for are pink and red. When am I?

I could feel the excitement rushing up and down of me. We were watching TV and waiting for the moment to happen. I never stayed up this late. It was really fun and in five seconds it would happen. 5,4,3,2,1. Once it happened everyone jumped up and down and cheered. I am the start of a long time. When am I?

I longed for the war to be over. Every morning, I would wake up to the sound of guns being fired. King George III kept claiming taxes on more and more things and we had no say in it. I felt like we were their slaves. The general was doing his best though. We hoped for the best for us. When am I?

I come to your house every year. I leave baskets for you with some candy and sometimes toys. I love one thing and that's eggs. Eggs are my favorite. Every year sometimes you try to catch me but I'm way too quick for you guys. You set up traps and cameras, but they never work on me. I always knock them down. Some people don't celebrate me. When am I?

ANSWER: Valentines Day (February 14)

ANSWER: New Year's Eve (December 31)

ANSWER: During the Revolutionary war period (1700s)

ANSWER: Easter (March or April)

My day is very important on the U.S. calendar. Schools close every year on my day. I'm celebrated because of special men from the past. These men did a great service for the United States of America. I'm celebrated in late winter every year. The first person to have the position being honored was named George. When am I?

Knights being knighted. Castles being attacked and defended. Legends of dragons ruling the sky. The chosen one slaying the beast. Hangings and executions. Kings sitting in golden thrones with a sword nearby. Plagues spreading like wildfire. When am I?

I am most kids' favorite day of the year. After 180 days of working, today is the day that will change. You may go on vacation, or just stay home. Kids are cleaning out their desks and heading home. Adults are very happy that I come. Kids have almost three months of relaxing. When am I?

I'm a land with no people. Just some crazy looking massive animals. I don't know where I am. I think I'm on Earth. I suddenly hear the ground shaking more and more. The gargantuan angry specimen was coming closer, and I started run. I didn't look back. It was big and scary. I hid and saw what it was doing. It was eating another big creature. When am I?

ANSWER: President's Day (third Monday in February)

ANSWER: Middle Ages (5th to 15th century)

ANSWER: Last day of school

ANSWER: Triassic or Jurassic time period (about 240 million years ago)

I am a national holiday. People have a huge feast on this day. They mostly eat turkey. The first year people celebrated me was in 1621. People are very grateful on this holiday. I am celebrated before winter begins in the United States. When am I?

I am a big holiday that is only celebrated in the U.S. I am in the summer season. It is only celebrated in the United States because it is the day we gained independence from Britain, and we became a new nation! It's a great time, and usually celebrated with fireworks. When am I?

Soldiers standing behind a stone wall with a musket and bayonet on the tip. Generals from two sides of the U.S stationed here. The argument out of hand. Neither side will negotiate. The army of the south. The army of the north. When one of the spies reported the Yankee climbing up Little Round Top, soldiers to help. When am I?

I am a holiday of red, pink, white, and other colors. I am a holiday of giving, but more loving. Hearts, cupid babies and much more! Some people go out on special places this day. When am I?

ANSWER: Thanksgiving (fourth Thursday in November in the U.S.)

ANSWER: Independence Day (July $)

ANSWER: The Civil War (1861-1865)

ANSWER: Valentine's Day (February 14)

Smoke blinded my eyes. The grass was splattered with specks of red. I hid with my attack dog behind debris of a building. Then I saw a Nazi soldier running towards me with a gun. Then he froze and fell over sideways. His doom had come. The horizon was a murky grey. I spotted a helmet next to me, it had a sign, a very bad sign that had two crosses that were overlapping each other, and I knew I had to escape. When am I?

I start with a generic word that many teachers do not like. This word is something that you would say to your dog, like "____ boy/girl". I am always on the same day of the week. I am considered a state holiday in twelve states. When am I?

I am a national holiday in the U.S.A. I celebrate people who served our country. Many schools have a ceremony for me. Everyone that I celebrate were in the military. Many people in the U.S. dress up in red, white, and blue for me. When am I?

I am another holiday that celebrates people. You may not realize it, but the people that I celebrate work very, very hard. Some give these people acknowledgements. Others give presents. These people provide knowledge and lessons to their students. When am I?

ANSWER: World War II (1939-1945)

ANSWER: Good Friday (the Friday before Easter)

ANSWER: Veterans Day (November 11)

ANSWER: Teacher Appreciation Day (Tuesday in first full week of May)

I am always on Tuesday. People get on the streets to celebrate me. There are usually floats, singing and dancing to celebrate me. I am before Ash Wednesday. Many people wear purple, green and gold for me. Some people call me Fat Tuesday. My name is in French.

You're happy on this day. If you're not then you should be. Everyone has their "own" day, but many people share the same day, too. You feel special and joyful. You can have a celebration with your friends and family on this day by eating cake or cupcakes. When am I?

An almost ancient city was calm with no hint of danger in the air. As destruction hit, townspeople were scrambling, trying to leave town. People were screaming and fleeing from the pieces of rock and ash. As the tides of ashes settled, many people were left petrified and dead. Fortunately, some people had survived the disaster that left the city in a preserved condition for almost 2,000 years. When am I?

I celebrate the freedom of a nation. The land that people who celebrate me were promised was founded as a nation in 1948. Slave masters were harassed by plagues, including darkness and frogs. The man that I mainly celebrate was not even let into the promised land for disobeying someone. I usually last eight days. When am I?

ANSWER: Mardi Gras (late winter – the day before Ash Wednesday)

ANSWER: Your birthday

ANSWER: Mt. Vesuvius Eruption (A.D.-C.E. 79)

ANSWER: Passover (early spring)

At this time you are probably eating. If you look outside you can see it is still bright out. Sometimes this takes place at noon, but it can be at any time. You have this at school. The food you are eating is probably much different than the first meal of the day. When am I?

I am one of the most joyous holidays in Jewish history. I celebrate a story many hundreds of years ago. My story took place in Ancient Persia. I am one of the only holidays where everyone shouts and make noises in the service at certain times. People customarily eat three sided cookies for me. They also dress up in costumes for me. When am I?

I am a day of happiness. I welcome a king, who came to his supporters riding a donkey. People threw branches that symbolized victory and peace. People make these branches into small items. I am the final day of a long period, and I am the start an important week. I am a day of obligation. The colors of this day are red and white, symbolizing the redemption in blood the king paid for the world. When am I?

I am a day that doesn't every year. Some people forget how important I am. I help the calendar year to go at the same rate as the solar year. I was "invented" back in the first century BC. I am in February. When am I?

ANSWER: Lunch time (mid-day)

ANSWER: Purim (late winter)

ANSWER: Palm Sunday (March or April)

ANSWER: February 29 (Leap Year)

We make dollies from corn leaves. We eat corn pancakes, and when they get cold they don't taste good anymore. We are very poor and we dress like pilgrims. We can only bathe in extremely cold water. We don't have cars or electronics. We don't even have televisions. We only have paintings. When am I?

I am not a national holiday. I am very fun to do, especially for children. Not everything is as it seems on my day. You really have to use brainpower to decipher a sentence said on my special day. I am celebrated on January 25. I can be very confusing, as not everyone could be celebrating me. Some people have their own celebration of me not on the traditional day. When am I?

I am a time that some students wait for at school with anticipation. Teachers love me. I am a break that takes up two days. Also, if your parents go to work they love me, too. You can do almost anything on me. You can watch a movie, stay up late, or have a sleepover. Most kids love me. When am I?

I am a time when most kids long for at school. It is up to the school district to decide how much or little they have of me. Parents might have me, too. You might go somewhere for me or might just stick around at your home. I can be in any season. I can be very little or very big. Not all schools or places have me. When am I?

ANSWER: Colonial times (1600s-1700s)

ANSWER: Opposite Day (January 25)

ANSWER: Weekend (Saturday and Sunday)

ANSWER: Vacation

I am near the Jewish holiday of Yom Kippur. I am a very joyous holiday for the Jewish people, a holiday of new beginnings. People blow a ram's horn on my day. They also eat apples dipped in honey, which makes me a children's' favorite. The Hebrew translation for me is literally "Head of the Year." When am I?

I can happen any day. People usually plan me at least a year in advance. I am usually the celebration of the making of a family. This day is something very important. Sometimes kids are invited and sometimes they're not. Most people take a vacation shortly after me. The parents usually get each other gifts such as rings, chocolate, flowers, and more. When am I?

I happen every month. I can get bright. I get big. I look like I am really close to you when look at me. I am in space. Lunar Eclipses only happen when I occur. I am not always this big when you see me. You see me in the sky. When mm I?

When you get to me some people say it's a dream that came true. Some people came to me many times, some people didn't. You may play a lot of games to get to me. You also could sweep every team. To get to me you need dominance and a hot streak. You could play up to 21 games to get to me, and you could play only 12 games to get to me. The West and East's best teams clash together in me. When am I?

ANSWER: Rosh Hashanah (September or October)

ANSWER: Wedding

ANSWER: Full Moon

ANSWER: NBA Finals

The first part people call me is a color. There are a lot of sales on this day from computers to simple card games. Stores are crowded on this day, and some people line up for hours to shop on my day. I am in November. The stores' opening hours for me are different for each store, but some open very early or stay open all night. When am I?

We try to wake up early and make a special person breakfast in bed. You cook them eggs and fill them a glass of orange juice. During the day you give them their cards and presents. You might surprise them with a fancy lunch and give them hugs and kisses. The day honors dads. When am I?

I am a Mexican holiday celebrated around the world. I am a three day event. One of those days is on Halloween. Many Mexicans celebrate their family and friends who passed away. Some people make sugar skulls. When am I?

I am standing at a big wall made of bags of sand. All of a sudden I heard something. It sounds like a train. My blood goes cold, I slide a bullet in my gun. There are 90 of us and 5,000 of them. We were under command of lieutenant John Chard and Gonville bromhead. We were fighting for the crown in the Anglo-Zulu war. When am I?

ANSWER: Black Friday (the day after Thanksgiving)

ANSWER: Father's Day (third Sunday in June)

ANSWER: Day of The Dead (October 31-November 2)

ANSWER: Rorkes Drift (1879)

I happen every once in awhile. I can be viewed from anywhere in the world. I last for a couple of hours. I happen when the moon passes directly behind the Earth, but the sun must align perfectly with the Earth as well. I can be called a blood moon. When am I?

I am a holiday, but I am a little controversial. Some of the time, kids get a day off of school or maybe adults get off of work. This day is celebrated in the fall. I am celebrated because a sailor with the first name of Christopher who discovered the Bahamas.Also, the capital of Ohio has the same name as this holiday. When am I?

Most Mexican people have a big celebration on my day. It honors the the battle won against France at the battle of Puebla during the Franco-Mexican war. Even though the Mexicans had a small army, it was at their hometown and they knew the place well, so they managed to defeat the French army. When am I?

This time is very important to your body. If you don't do the things you are doing during this time properly, you can get seriously injured. If you do me correctly you can get injured, but there is less chance of getting injured later. If you perform me correctly, you will do better in your sport. You can play games during me, but some people might not do that because they do not want to be injured. These stretches you do during me are very good for you. When am I?

ANSWER: Lunar Eclipse

ANSWER: Columbus Day (second Monday in October)

ANSWER: Cinco de Mayo (May 5)

ANSWER: Pregame Warm-ups/Stretching

I happened about 87 years after the Patriots won the Revolutionary War. Some people like to reference me as 4×20+7 years after. One of the most famous U.S. presidents said a speech on my day, which made my date famous. This president was not only known for his life, but also for his death. He is on two types of U.S. currency. In the first four words two numbers were said. When am I?

Today is the day to celebrate by giving your mom gifts and love. Kiss her, hug her, thank her, and much more. You usually buy her some kind of flower. Flower sales are huge on my day. You can also go out for dinner just for your mom. Support her with love on this day. When am I?

I was so exciting. In effect, the atmosphere was burning with excitement. All of a sudden, the blasters went off and the landing slowed. Everyone was on the verge of happiness. Then three, two, one, landing. The crowd went up in cheers. I was the first U.S. spacecraft on Mars. When am I?

I am a very sad time, which also revolutionized a way of transportation. I was very unexpected. People cheered before I happened. Seven people died because of me. I looked like I spontaneously combusted, but instead, part of me was leaking, and that fluid caught fire. I exploded after being in air for 76 seconds. There were multiple recordings of me. A teacher was onboard. When am I?

ANSWER: Gettysburg Address (November 19, 1863)

ANSWER: Mother's Day (second Sunday of May)

ANSWER: Landing of Viking 1 (July 20, 1976)

ANSWER: Space Shuttle Challenger Explosion (January 28, 1986)

This happens in June. Some celebrate this to give faith, hope, love, and commitment to children ages 1-18. This is a national holiday. Not many know about this day. But you will, because when you see the answer you will find out! But it is very different from other holidays. Remember, few celebrate this. When am I?

I am a very important event. I occur every four years. There is a decision you can make before this day to get prepared. People are either mad, happy, or don't care when I end. Most countries have me. If the world didn't have me, some things would be different. When am I?

Jake was running around screaming. He was on Breed's Hill, and there were so many loud noises. There were many things flying in the air. Jake ran into a tree and got knocked out unconscious. One hour later he started to regain consciousness. When he looked up he saw five big men in ripped, red suits, and they were holding muskets and glooming over him. It was 1775. When am I?

ANSWER: Children's Day (second Sunday in June)

ANSWER: Election Day (the first Tuesday after November 1, in the U.S.)

ANSWER: Battle of Bunker Hill (June 17, 1775)

Where Am I?

Where Am I?

The bed was still cold as well as the air. The musty smell never went away. I knew even if I tried to get rid of them they would be back. The thick, cold, metal bars were blocking my view. I knew it would be a long time until I left the place I am calling home. I shouldn't have done what I did. Where am I?

I am known to have a logo with six of the same object. I am fluidly full of people roaming around me, choosing which ride to go on. You can find me around the USA. I have rides named after some super heroes in the Batman series. I have some people hired to sell ice cream for the people and to keep them busy. I am also known for having water slides. Where am I?

As I walked in, the bells rang over my head. I saw a bunch of sugary goodness. I decided to pick a yummy treat so I went to the cashier and paid for the treat. It was only a dollar. All around me were colorful things that kids love. I went home while eating all my sweets. Where am I?

The wind hit my face like a never ending wave of air. I heard low pitched growls coming from under me, and songs were blaring out of the speakers with an occasional advertisement. The trees and glass was blurry as well as the cement on the ground. Yellow stripes decorated the ground as well as a rare white. I put my head back and looked into the sky. Where am I?

ANSWER: Prison/Jail

ANSWER: Six flags

ANSWER: Candy Store

ANSWER: In a Car

I looked at the uneven steps as well as the cobwebs that were piling up. A raggedy doll stared at me silently with beady stalking eyes. A shadow ran right in front of my eyes, but there was nothing in sight. A spider crawled into a dark rotting corner. It looked like no one was here for a long time. Then I saw another shadow, which was shaped in a person wearing a very long cape. Where am I?

I see wide, tall, colorful buildings everywhere made of glass and metal. The smell of beef and soy fills the air. People with sparkles and paint on their faces walk around. Flags of blue, red, white, and black wave around in the air. People in robes dance as people clap, yell and throw money into a hat or jar. In the distance I could see the Yellow Sea. Where am I?

I walk down the uneven brick road. I look to the left and see an ancient battleground with wrecked buildings and stone everywhere. The short buildings are so close together - almost as they all were one. In the distance the water is shining and reflecting the sun, which was about to set. I walk into a restaurant, which sits on the edge of the Gulf of Mexico, and the smell of beans, rice, and beef fills the air. I see a waiter bring tacos to a family. Where am I?

I am in a desert in the United States. You can't visit here, so some people say it's one of the hardest places to enter. Aliens are said to be here. I am located in Lincoln County, Nevada. A lot of UFO reports have been seen here. Where am I?

ANSWER: Haunted House

ANSWER: South Korea

ANSWER: Mexico

ANSWER: Area 51

As I walked in through the door, I heard peaceful music coming from the back of the room. I saw a waitress coming and asking us "How many people are eating today sir?" My father answered, "four people." The waitress said to follow her and pointed at a table for us to sit at, and gave us a menu. Where am I?

A guy points to the problem on the board. "What is this?" he asks. The room is silent. I stare at the desk and work it around in my head. This one is very hard. Even worse, I need to remember it for an important test. Where am I?

The seven spikes are beautiful. As the daylight burns away, the torch seemed to light up the New York City sky Then suddenly a group of people come rushing out. I heard a little bit of their conversation. They said, "Hey Max, isn't she beautiful?" Then they walked away. Where am I?

The crowd goes wild as the receiver catches the ball. It's on now! He jukes a player and another person stopped. It wasn't enough to keep the play going. The ball soars through the air to the man back deep on the field. He catches it and starts running. 15 yards, then the 20, then the 40, the 50, then the 40! He's finally stopped. Where am I?

ANSWER: Restaurant

ANSWER: Classroom

ANSWER: Statue of Liberty

ANSWER: Football game

I am a dangerous place located in the Atlantic Ocean. I have a nickname of "Devil's Triangle." I am located from San Juan, Puerto Rico to Miami, Florida to Bermuda. Most people and vehicles get lost in me. I am one of the world's most mysterious places. Where Am I?

My mom walks, shoes clacking on the tiled floor, casually picking up items. "Why had I come with her on this?" I think. "Ooh, those look good," I say, pointing a green cardboard package. "I think this is what you need," mom says, picking up a different one. "No eew, oatmeal raisin that one tastes bad." This had been a mistake, and a boring one. Where am I?

I am a part of the United States of America. Some sharks are here because of the warm water. One of the most famous theme parks in the world is here. Thousands of people each winter come here to for the warm weather instead of staying up north. I am nicknamed the Sunshine State because I have a lot of sunshine. The capital of me is Tallahassee. Where am I?

I am a great place to go on a hot day. When you are all hot, sticky and sweaty, I may cool you off. Some people like to take bike rides on me to places. I can be very dangerous to people and homes when there are bad storms. You can find me around the coast of the country you live in. I am a great place to go when you want to relax. I am always there, and always will be. Where am I?

ANSWER: Bermuda Triangle

ANSWER: Grocery Store

ANSWER: Florida

ANSWER: Beach

The beautiful sunset made the building look colorful and picturesque. The building was only white though. As I stepped in the big corridor, I saw lines of people walking alone or in groups. As I walked out, I stopped to gaze at four huge pillars holding nothing. The number of workers took to build me was 20,000. I am one of the seven wonders of the world. I am located in Asia. Where am I?

In the corner of my eye, I could see kids on equipment, laughing. Some people were sitting, some were standing, and even more were running. As my teacher blew the whistle I knew it was time to go inside. Where am I?

This was very hard to get used to, but I kept reminding myself that I was about to go where very few human has gone before. I finally put myself down on the seat and put on my elaborate seatbelt. The launch was rough, but eventually I could see the moon grow in size. I felt like I was a feather. Where am I?

You hear people of all ages. You see lines everywhere. People are carrying sodas, lemonades, and even ice cream. You get in a long line and when it's your turn you put the harness over your head. You start to move fast and you go up a huge hill. You hear click after click until you reach the top. Where am I?

ANSWER: Taj Mahal

ANSWER: Recess at school

ANSWER: In a space shuttle

ANSWER: Amusement park

I am home to many fun rides. One famous ride is called Splash Mountain, but there is much, much, more. A lot of people come visit me in Florida for vacation. I am home to many famous characters. One of them is Mickey Mouse. I am made up of four theme parks. Where am I?

They are doing an activity that is known to be one of the most played activities in the U.S. While I watch, the other people watching do, or try to do a wave. The other people also cheer and make chants. I see men recording the game. It sometimes gets televised nationally. This activity is a sport played ten players at a time. The people playing are on a court. Where am I?

As I walked through the grass, I had a bunch of choices. To play on the swings, the slide, or the rock wall. I wanted to swing so I went to the swing and I asked my mom to push me. After about 30 minutes we went back home. Where am I?

Some people say that I'm the "wonder of the world." A lot of people love to see me and take photos of me. they say I am so "rich and "elegant." I am an Incan citadel set high in the Andes Mountains in Peru, above the Urubamba River valley. I was built in the 15th century and later abandoned. I have dry-stones walls, and intriguing buildings that play on astronomical alignments and panoramic views. I was also a lost city. Where am I?

ANSWER: Disney World

ANSWER: Basketball Game

ANSWER: Park

ANSWER: Machu Picchu

I turn on my light and start reading my book. Blankets and pillows comforting me, I grab my little teddy bear. I put my book away, close my eyes and shut off the lights. Where am I?

I shivered with fear. "Have fun!" yelled my mom as she drove away. It was the first day of summer and I am getting tortured again. The activities were for babies, and the lake was shallow and cold. When I tried to eat my sandwich bees circled my head. Laying down in my cabin that first night I was a bit homesick. As I was shutting my eyes all the mosquitos attacked. I was getting eaten alive! Where am I?

I am pretty well known by a lot of people. I am very long, I'm about 5,500 miles long! People started to build me as early as 7th century BC. Walls like me were built and then added all together to make one big, giant, long, wall. Where am I?

As I am getting on I see the water touching the land. We start moving outwards. I stick my hands in a bucket of worms and I put one on the hook. I lower the rod into the body of water and wait. I wait until I feel a tug on the rod. The liquid was rocking back and forth. Where am I?

ANSWER: In a bed

ANSWER: Sleep away summer camp

ANSWER: The Great Wall of China

ANSWER: On a fishing boat

If you are a kid then you come here many days in a week. Well, most kids do. If you are older than you would wake up earlier to go here. But if you are younger then lucky you, you get to sleep in! This place is in your town or city, so it's easy to get to. You learn and have fun here. Where am I?

I am on a planet - the sixth one from the sun. I am on the second largest one, after Jupiter. I have 62 moons that orbit around me, many of which are named after greek figures. Rings encircle me. I am on a gas giant that is about nine times earth's size. Where am I?

I am a tall object in the sky. It's cold and snowy, and I sit in the center of Nepal. Reaching the top of where I am is a challenging task, and few people have completed it. Some have even died trying to succeed. But if you get to the top it is a tremendous accomplishment. I am actually not the tallest mountain in the world. The place I am on is one of the natural wonders of the world. Where am I?

I am in a place with a lot history and great architectural design. The Notre Dame Cathedral is located in me. You can buy delicious crepes to eat. You could see the Eiffel Tower, and Napoleon's tomb. The Louvre is another famous palace here. Where am I?

ANSWER: School

ANSWER: Saturn

ANSWER: Mount Everest

ANSWER: Paris, France

I am in a country located in southern Asia. The Tropic of Cancer runs through the northern part of me. I am in a land of diverse culture, with festivals and celebrations almost every month. In 2017 it had a population of 1.252 billion people! My main religion is Hinduism. This country was under the rule of the mughal empire for some time, and then was under the British. Where am I?

I am a lost place in this world. Everyone who lived here disappeared leaving no evidence except a single skeleton and the word "Croatoan" carved into wood. More than 100 people vanished. There are many theories about what happened. One of the stories happened to be that the Spaniards killed them. I was the first British colony in North America. Now, a town in North Carolina has the same name as me. Where am I?

I am near the equator. I am considered a tropical paradise. I am filled with clear water and palm trees. I am located in the Northern Hemisphere. I have my own language. I am a great place for a vacation. I was made by underwater volcanoes, and I am in the U.S. Where am I?

I kneel down on the pew and start saying prayers. When I'm done, I leave the building and hop into my car. I remember that I forgot to take the holy water on my way out. On Sunday, I will go back into the building and pray that I'll be forgiven. Where am I?

ANSWER: India

ANSWER: Roanoke (North Carolina)

ANSWER: Hawaii

ANSWER: Church

Most people have heard about me, but have never gone there. No one really talks about me. I have animals that people like. My climate is very unique. There are many sea creatures under and around me. I am very pesky on the globe or a flat map because of my location. Usually if people think about me they think cold and white. Where am I?

I am a planet. One very big invasion took place on me. I am snowy and have many unique creatures on my surface. They include the wampa and the tauntaun. I was in the movie "Star Wars." The Rebel Alliance used to have a base on me. When the Empire forced them off me I was sad. Obi-Wan Kenobi made an appearance to Luke Skywalker as a ghost on me. Where am I?

I was finished in 1856 after taking 34 years to build. I am a very big tower and a huge tourist attraction. There is a big clock at the top of me. I can't believe that I am 16 stories high and also 315 feet tall. My first and last name both start with B's. Where am I?

As I walk through the sand, my feet felt smooth. My dad put up the big umbrella and my mom took a rest on a chair. I put down my towel and slowly go into the water. Where am I?

ANSWER: Antarctica

ANSWER: Hoth

ANSWER: Big Ben

ANSWER: Beach

I am finally in line to see a famous landmark located in Pennsylvania. It's made out of many materials like copper, zinc, and gold. It weighs an astonishing 2,080 pounds. Millions of people visit the gargantuan chime each year. It is a symbol of American independence. Where am I?

I am riding across this famous structure. The color of this landmark is declared "International Orange." It is 2,737 meters long holding more than 800,000 tons. The American Society of Civil Engineers calls this one of the wonders of the world. It ends in Marin County starting at the northern tip of a peninsula located in the most populated state in the U.S. Where am I?

There are different types of me. I can be large or small. I may be recently made or the opposite. I can be filthy or very clean. I have things that are probably important to you. I'm a place that you know about. You live in me. Where am I?

The floor creaked beneath me as I paced around. I looked outside, and a stray branch blocked my view. I found jagged splinters on my hands as well as my feet. Rain came pouring down, but I wasn't wet. I was surprised that the roof wasn't leaking water. Then I realized I needed to put a window in. All this hard work was paying off. Where am I?

ANSWER: Liberty Bell

ANSWER: Golden Gate Bridge

ANSWER: Your home

ANSWER: In a tree house

I am usually for the entire town to share. I am usually outdoors, and when I am outdoors, I am closed for the winter, yet open when it's hot. I almost always have people in me, which is full of chlorine so I can kill germs. I have people relaxing near me on a sunny day on chairs. Some people bring in toys to play with, such as ducks, floating donuts, and other fun toys meant to play with in me. Where am I?

I am very loud and noisy. I have many people on me such as a stewardess and a captain. There are many seats on me. Sometimes I even have televisions. There are usually some people serving food for you. I have a lot of small windows. I very rarely crash, and I am much safer than a car. Where am I?

I am somewhere big. There are honking horns everywhere. Birds are everywhere. Stores, restaurants, and apartments are in me. Some people live on the streets. There are a lot of big things surrounding me. There are a lot of street lights and street signs. There are also a lot of hotels. Where am I?

I was up so high that I could see the town below. I am puffy and sometimes filled with liquid. Sometimes my liquid gushes out on the people below. Planes can fly through me. Where am I?

ANSWER: Pool

ANSWER: Airplane

ANSWER: City

ANSWER: Cloud

I am a major tourist attraction. I live in England. Nobody knows what my purpose is. I am a very well known wonder of the world. People started to construct me in 3200 B.C. I was built in phases. There are reports of UFOs sighted above me. People have festivals for me. Where am I?

I am at an annual convention held in San Diego, California. The first time this event took place it was a three-day event, from August 1 to August 3 in 1970. The first time it happened it was held in the basement of the U.S. Grant hotel. In 2015, about 167,000 people attended! There are exhibits everywhere about famous comics! Where am I?

I am a body of water that is 1,946 feet deep. A lot of tourists visit this landmark each year. I was created by a volcano exploding and collapsing. The islands that are close to where I am now are Wizard Island and Phantom Ship. I am the deepest lake in the USA and am located in Oregon. Where am I?

ANSWER: Stonehenge

ANSWER: Comic-Con

ANSWER: Crater Lake

What Am I?

If everyone recycled me, we would save about 250 million trees each year. A lot of studies show I am the most effective place to advertise store sales and promotions. 99.4% of all retailers advertise their business in me. I can be written in many different languages. I am mostly black & white. What am I?

People scuba dive in the ocean to find me. Some people like to take me as a souvenir, but they're not supposed to. I am usually found in tropical places. I am usually red, blue, pink, yellow, purple, and green. Even fish live in me, but you can also get cut on me. Sometimes trash gets stuck in me and I get destroyed. What am I?

People sometimes need me on very hot days. I can be plugged into the wall, battery operated, or hand worked. Sometimes I hang on the ceiling. I'm used mostly in the summer. I blow a lot of air around in the area I am in. There are many types of me. What am I?

I am a fighter space ship. I have parallel wings with a cockpit in the center of the lines. My pilots wear all black and white pilot gear. I fight against other ships that are X's and many more. I'm from a galaxy far, far away. What am I?

ANSWER: Newspaper

ANSWER: Sea coral

ANSWER: Fan

ANSWER: TIE Fighter (from *Star Wars*)

My inside is hollow. I am the most important bone in your body. If you break the living version of me, it will be catastrophic, and you will need to go to the hospital. Let's just say I'm the bodyguard of the brain. I also hold your eyes, ears, nose, and mouth. Most organisms have me. I am also used for decorations on a certain holiday. I am derived from "Old Norse," a Latin word. What am I?

I am a building block that you have to put a lot time into in order for me to be complete. I don't have to be built into one thing and one thing only. I can be a space ship, a big fort, or just some wacky creation. There is even a video game based off of me, as well as a movie. Sometimes you can buy me in a set of 1,000, and I'm not just bricks, I can be little people, too. What am I?

I am an animal. Some people think I am red but I am can be different colors. I can live up to 2-5 years. There are 5 different species of me. You may have me living in your backyard. In Japanese, I am a Kitsune. The Chinese believe that I am a spirit. What am I?

There are lots of companies who make me. I am usually a rectangle shape. I can be held easily in one hand. Most adults have me, and most kids don't have me. I have a weird number on the face of me because of security. You can use me to buy things. What am I?

ANSWER: Skull

ANSWER: Legos

ANSWER: Fox

ANSWER: Credit Card

You may use me if you have at school presentations. I can be really big or teeny tiny. I am used usually for science fairs. I can attract a lot of people. I was created in 1796. I often have words and pictures on me. I am usually made of a hard paper. You may have one of me hanging in your room. What am I?

If you didn't have me for a long time, you would die. I have a lot of companies that sell me in bottles. I can be a habitat for animals. 71 percent of me is on Earth's surface. One place might have more of me than another. My scientific name is Oxidane. What am I?

I am a picture, but there is something special about me. My inventor was Steve Wilhite. Google calls me a different name than my original name. The name everyone calls for me actually stands for something. I am a picture, but I move. You might see me in a digital presentation. What am I?

Some people like me, and some dislike me. I have many brands that make me. There are some major brands out there that make me. The two foods I am flavored as are bitter fruits. Both the foods are very healthy though. Some people don't have me because I can be bad for you. You can drink me. What am I?

ANSWER: Poster board

ANSWER: Water

ANSWER: GIF (Graphic Interchange Format)

ANSWER: Lemon-Lime Soda

I can be funny, but I might not be. I can be printed on paper and can be on a screen. There are many channels dedicated for me. There are simple, and plain, but funny ones of me and some other ones can be very complex. Émile Cohl made the first of me in 1908. I am made up of things some people love to do. I can be used for learning and many other reasons. I am 2-D. What am I?

People made me a very long time ago. In fact, I was first made in the B.C time period. Also, people think I originate from Mexico. I am rich in calories and have many health benefits. I have two names, which many people know. People can make biofuels from me because of a chemical I have. I am used for eating, feeding animals, and much more. I can range in many different colors. What am I?

I usually come in a bottle. I can be many different colors. Some examples of these are pastel pink, blue, white, beige and many, many more. You usually use me after you take a shower or when your skin is dry. You put me all over your body, but not usually on your face. They make a special kind of me for your face. What am I?

I am fluffy and stuffed. I can be found in your home, often in several rooms. I can be in any color or pattern you choose. You love having fights with me at sleepovers. I can be sat on. I can be decorative. I am usually made of fabric and filled with cotton, feathers, or any other soft materials. What am I?

ANSWER: Cartoons

ANSWER: Corn

ANSWER: Lotion

ANSWER: Pillow

Many people drink me around the world. Some examples of me are Red Bull, Monster, and Rockstar. Skateboarders and race car drivers sometimes are sponsored by many brands of me. I have 74 milligrams of caffeine in some of my drinks. I am not that healthy, but people drink me at certain times when they need me. What am I?

In World War I, I was mistakenly recommended as a food source in Britain. This was a mistake because my leaves can potentially be deadly, as they contain a certain type of acid. My base can be very delicious, if sweetened, that is. I can be very sour. I can be particularly delicious in pies. I appeared in the TV show *Chopped* as a deadly ingredient. What am I?

I am connected to a strong stem. I grow under dirt and it takes a long time for me to grow. You wash me before cooking me so I'm not dirty. I'm green and I look wrinkly. There are many different ways to cook me. Some people don't want to eat me because they don't like my taste. I am a vegetable. What am I?

I am very important wherever I live. Some of my kind can live for up to eight years! I can be 22 feet long, but typically I average about 7-8 centimeters. Some scary creatures like to snack on me. Having me in a habitat is very good, you may think I am disgusting the way I help the environment, but I am very useful. Fishermen really like me. What am I?

ANSWER: Energy Drink

ANSWER: Rhubarb

ANSWER: Kale

ANSWER: Worm

I can be all different colors, but blue or red are the most popular. I can make a huge mess that parents usually hate. I go in a box that has something fragile. I stick to things when I'm wet. I also get soggy and sticky when I am touched. I am made of corn starch. You can play many games with me. What am I?

I am a drink that is named after a famous golfer. I am mixed with something sour and something sweet. I am usually cold. Some people may not know the name of me, but a lot of people like to drink me. I could be the color pink, orange, or yellow. What am I?

I can be big. The wind moves me by pushing me where I want to go. Some people enjoy going on me, but other people dislike going on me. Some people get sick on me. I have a manual motor on me that goes really slow. I am compound word. What am I?

Some people travel all over with me. Others keep me in a secure location. Wherever they put me, they don't want to lose me as I keep track of something very valuable. I can be many different colors. I am usually issued from the bank. I can be used to pay for things as an alternative for cash. What am I?

ANSWER: Playing cards

ANSWER: Arnold Palmer (Drink)

ANSWER: Sailboat

ANSWER: Checkbook

Most of the time, I have important stuff on me. It can be difficult to put things on me. I come in many designs and can be a souvenir. I can soft or hard. I can be thick or thin. I might come from a business or be on display. The person who invented me was Frederick J. Loudin. I can come in different sizes and shapes. What am I?

You may not always notice me. I keep what's inside of me safe from melting or getting sticky, or for keeping me clean. Sometimes I am made out of wax-paper or plastic. Sometimes I am easy to open and sometimes not. Kids love what's inside me. My design can be plain or my design can be catchy. What am I?

I am shimmery and shiny. I come in sticks or other things. I am often red, but I come in other colors, too. People use me to look pretty. Kids sometimes wear me if their parents allow them to. I am used for your lips. I am mostly used by women and girls. What am I?

I am a little item you hang in a car. I am sometimes shaped to look like a plant. I come in different colors. You usually want me in an automobile. I can be deadly. I can cause headaches, dizziness and other negative symptoms from me. I can increase the risk of asthma in children. Canadian-born chemist Julius Sämann invented me. What am I?

ANSWER: Keychain

ANSWER: Candy wrapper

ANSWER: Lip Gloss

ANSWER: Air Freshener

I am small with sharp little edges around the top of me. I am the head of something you drink out of. A lot of people think I will be money if there is ever a apocalypse or a nuclear war. People have collections of me from many years ago. I am made in factories around the world. What am I?

There are lots of different brands that make me. I can be one color or multiple colors. I am usually used during summer or in warm places. You might not want to wear me when it's cold. I was used regularly by Egyptians. I'm used in many countries. I can be for all genders and for all ages, and I go on your feet. What am I?

I am a type of berry, but most people don't know that. In some places they call me a plantain. I can be red, green, brown, or yellow. My scientific name is musa sapientum. I grow on a tree, mostly in tropical areas. I am tasty with peanut butter. Most people think that I am a monkey's favorite food. What am I?

The world uses about 200 million of me every year. I am made with aluminum. What's inside of me is bad for you if you drink too much. Some people throw me out instead of properly disposing of me. I contain a great taste. A lot of people like what is inside of me. What am I?

ANSWER: Bottle Cap

ANSWER: Sandals

ANSWER: Banana

ANSWER: Soda can

I am a liquid applied to your hair after shampooing. I make your hair softer and lighter. Sometimes people forget to apply me on their hair. If that's true, after they get out of the shower, their hair will not be soft. It's like a haystack. I'm most important to use in the winter. What am I?

I am a spring vegetable. If I am boiled I have 20 calories, if I am not then I have three calories. I have vitamin A and C. I am mostly green. I am long and skinny. I have "spikes" on me. I have a little brush on my tip. 72 percent of the world like this vegetable. I am a relative of brussel sprouts. What am I?

I am a vegetable. You can grow me. I can be eaten cooked or raw. I have some green on me. If you don't include the green part of me, I am round at the top, with a pointy bottom. I can be any size. If you consume me, I can help your eyesight. I am usually orange. What am I?

I can be used for many different things, including magic tricks, games, and more. There are a lot of types of me. I am either black or red. I have other colors on some of me. This is only on specific ones though. I come with exactly 52 of me. What am I?

ANSWER: Packing Peanuts

ANSWER: Conditioner

ANSWER: Asparagus

ANSWER: Cards

Some people love me. I am sometimes pure squeezed. Some people drink me in the morning for breakfast. Sometimes people make me at their house. People of all ages drink me. What am I?

If you don't use me people will usually think you're very weird, disgusting, crazy, and more. You can donate me to places where they accept things like me. Some people rip me while playing sports. Jacob W. Davis invented me. You probably have a few of me. Most people tend to use the short ones of me in the summer, and in the winter people tend to use the long ones. What am I?

You might use me often, or never use me at all. The person who invented me was Nikola Tesla. I can be used to control various types of things. I have buttons, which are like commands, to make the object that I am controlling work. These can change depending on what I control. I have developed many features over the years. What am I?

I am a source of light for camping or party decorations. You hold me or carry me around you neck or wrist. You may freeze me to make me last longer but there is a danger of me exploding in your freezer. I can be all sorts of different colors purple, blue, yellow, and many other colors. What is inside of me is poisonous so don't eat me. What am I?

ANSWER: Orange Juice

ANSWER: Pants

ANSWER: Remote control

ANSWER: Glow stick

I am common on the side of the road. I used to have a wax candle in me. I am on at night, and off at day. I am usually made of mercury. I usually have a solar dial in me. There are wind powered versions of me. There is a song with my name in it. What am I?

I am an essential part of your everyday life even though you may not realize it. I am very popular in rural areas. I am a part of what keeps all humans alive with my oxygen. I was here before humans existed. Many things are made from me, including paper. What am I?

I can come in any form. I can hold water and plants. I can be very colorful. I usually come in various colors. I am mostly made of regular clay, but sometimes I am made out of glass. I can be for plants or just decor. I can sometimes even be hanged and used as lights. What am I?

I can be big, small or pretty much every size and shape. I am a place to store crispy treats. Some children try to sneak a bite of what's in me when their parents aren't looking. A lot of people love what is inside me, especially if they are craving a round treat. What am I?

ANSWER: Streetlight

ANSWER: Tree

ANSWER: Vase

ANSWER: A cookie jar

I was born in the 17th Century in Turkey. I am very useful, and there are many types of me. I can be made out of flimsy material, strong material, and many, many more. Most people use the strong and rough kind of me. I am used for a variety of reasons, but mainly I am used for absorbing water. Most people have me, but some people don't. What am I?

There are millions and millions of me. I am on any kind of device. I can be on a lot of different types of topics like cheese, animals, holidays, etc. I can be very popular or unpopular. The first one of me was created by a human named Tim Berners-Lee. You go to me often when you are online. What am I?

You can buy me at the store or make your own. I can be made out of different material. I can be used as a disguise. I am used in some sports. I can be different colors and represent different things. I might even have a purpose. Usually, when you wear me, you have little circles for your eyes. Some people use me for Halloween. What am I?

Many people like me, but the people who don't like me usually dislike me very strongly. I can have many vegetables in me as well as meat. There are a few ingredients you need to make me. Vinegared rice is one of them. I can be an appetizer or a main dish. There are many restaurants that have me on the menu. What am I?

ANSWER: Towel

ANSWER: Website

ANSWER: Mask

ANSWER: Sushi

I hold your clothes, hats, gloves, etc. I have a hook on the top. I am made out of wire, wood, plastic and SO many other things. I am not heavy (in weight). I can be sharp or spiky, but other than that, I am pretty safe. What am I?

I come in many different colors, but the most common color is black. There are very expensive ones of me and there are cheap ones of me. I am a common writing utensil in schools. I can be very complex and have many features to make me operate correctly. László Bíró was my inventor. What am I?

I hold a salty sauce. I am a bag-like object. I tear easily so you can pour the sauce on your food. You don't use the sauce on all types of foods. I can hold the sauce packet. This liquid inside of me, is brownish-blackish. I can go on sushi, but remember... not too much because I am salty. What am I?

I represent something of a country or a group. I can be big or I can be very small. Either way, I am usually important. When people think of me some people think where they live or where they were born. I can be colorful or I can be dull. Famous ones of me are usually very symbolic. When armies go into war they usually use me. When a person designs me for an important thing they usually put a lot of symbols of the important thing on me as well as putting a lot of effort into me. What am I?

ANSWER: Hanger

ANSWER: Pen

ANSWER: Soy sauce packet

ANSWER: Flag

I have many names. I can contain a lot of information, although I can have limited space based on the type of me. You can buy me in different sizes and different amounts of storage. I can be used to show presentations, or essays on different computers, laptops, and many more devices. I can also be used for backup storage. What am I?

I can be given to toddlers, and can be given to adults. They both can be happy if they receive me. I make the people who get me proud because that means they did something good. I am sometimes made of several. Each color usually means something. I can be worth a very large amount of money and I can be worth a small amount of money. What am I?

I am yellow, but I can be different colors, too. I am a toy that floats on water. Sometimes I can suck up water and squirt it out if you give me a big squeeze. Sometimes I even make a squeaking noise if you squeeze me. I'm an animal that is a land and water animal. I'm made out of rubber, and I'm a common toy for babies in a bathtub. What am I?

I am a fast sprouter. I am 89% water. I contain vitamins A, C, and K. I am usually harvested when I am 1½-5 inches tall, but I can grow up to two feet. I am usually used for soups and sandwiches for my tangy flavor. I am an edible herb. What am I?

ANSWER: USB Drive

ANSWER: Medal

ANSWER: Rubber duck

ANSWER: Garden cress

I go back and forth. I am like a piece of playground equipment. Part of me can be used in a vehicle. I live on a tree, usually in the front or back of your yard. Usually children sit on me. People spin me when they use me. What am I?

I drill holes through wood and other materials that you want to drill holes in. My motor is very powerful. I go up or down based on how deep you want to drill. I was created in 1889 by Arthur James Arnot and William Blanch. I can also be used with a vice. What am I?

I can be used for many different things, including magic tricks, games and more. There are a many types of me. I have different colors in some of me but I am mostly either black or red. I come with 52 in a pack. What am I?

I am one of the most well known instruments in the world. I was invented in 1655. There are also a lot of different formats of me. I am pretty big. I'm a very common instrument. I can make low notes or high notes. My keys are sometimes made out of ebony and ivory. My base is usually made out of wood and painted over. What am I?

ANSWER: Tire swing

ANSWER: Drill press

ANSWER: Playing cards

ANSWER: Piano

I am everywhere. I can be said in many ways. You might have different purposes to use me. If you didn't know I existed, life would be very hard. Once you use me, you can't take me back. There are many different kinds of me from different places. There are 171,476 in the English language. What am I?

I am used for a lot of games. Most of time, I have sand in me. It depends on how much sand that I have that will make me stay longer on the top. It can be different for different types. I can be used to keep track of time or just for fun. I was invented around 150 B.C. My sand can be different colors. I have different purposes. What am I?

I am an old invention used for cooling. I was first made in 3000 B.C, during the dynasty time. I can have a design or be plain. I was used by warriors as a weapon. I can be made out of paper, bronze, or silver. I was a toy people would give to children a long time ago. I am often made in China and Japan. What am I?

I'm a helpful invention. People don't think of me when they use me sometimes because they are so used to using me. I can be expensive or cheap. I let you read at certain times of the day. I can be used for many different things. I have endless styles. If I wasn't around, you'd probably have to go back to using candles. What am I?

ANSWER: Words

ANSWER: Hourglass

ANSWER: Hand Fan

ANSWER: Lamp

I have legs, but I can't use them by myself. You probably use me at work or at school. I can be made out of many materials like wood, metal, plastic, glass, and much more! I am used for many things like to work on, for putting on makeup, for doing school work on, and much more. Most types of me can hold things but some can't. Some can even have shelves and built in fish tanks! I usually come with a chair. What am I?

I am a very useful material. People don't use as much electricity during the day because of me. I am less useful at night. If you don't have me on your house you would be wasting lots of money on your electricity bill. You can also put a drink in me. I can be part of a bottle or a window. What am I?

I am a green food. People love to sometimes cut me up and put me in soup. I am a vegetable from a marshland plant. I am very crunchy. I have an excellent source of vitamin K. Some people do not like me, but I go great with chicken wings. I am the main part of the snack called *Ants on a log*. What am I?

I am made to seal something. You need to use a tool to pull me out. I am hard. I can be big or small. My size depends on what I must seal. I get stained by a drink that is red. I am made out of a bark's tissue. I am used to seal bottles. What am I?

ANSWER: Desk

ANSWER: Glass

ANSWER: Celery

ANSWER: Cork

I am like a book, but I have a major difference. I can have all kinds of different places and things and me that you choose. You decide on everything in me. I might even have words. I come in a lot of different colors. I can be big or small. I can be events that happened to you in the past. I have pictures of memories in me. What am I?

I am a plant. My scientific name is Menthae. I belong to the family of Lamiaceae. I often grow quickly. I can be stored in a plastic bag in the fridge. Some people eat me plain and some people like to add me in their salads or tea. I am a popular gum and tea flavor. What am I?

I am made out of dairy. I come in all sorts of shapes, sizes, colors, and types. I can be hard or soft, squishy or not, or sweet or spicy. I sit out in a room for about year. I am in a lot of different types of foods like casseroles, pastas, and more. I may smell really good or smell like garbage. What am I?

I am something you constantly use, almost every day. You use me in school, work, and at home. I am a tool that allows you to search things up, watch videos, do homework, pay bills, and talk to friends. I became popular in 1990, but now almost everyone uses me. You probably used me just a few minutes ago. What am I?

ANSWER: Photo album

ANSWER: Mint

ANSWER: Cheese

ANSWER: The internet

I am a food you will find in a specific type of restaurant. I originated from Portuguese missionaries and merchants in the sixteenth century. They introduced me to a country on the Asian coast. I am a deep fried vegetable or fish. I was founded in 1549. What am I?

I am usually made out of metal or wood. I am a tool that can be used for gardening. I have a sharp blade at one end of me. I have a wooden stick and then a metal sheet attached to it. I can be used for lifting coal, gravel, and other pieces of stone. What am I?

I can be low to the ground or high up, but I am resting on poles. Some people can reach me while standing on the ground and some can't. It depends on if I am standing tall or short. Some people think it is more fun to play on top of me if they can't reach me standing on the ground. People usually complete me in a pattern. They swing with one hand and then reach for the next metal\beam, and then hold on and then swing. What am I?

I am a very useful item used with a popular electronic product. People use me to do something. I can be flat or raised. Christopher Latham Sholes invented me first. I come in many different brands. The alphabet is on me. What am I?

ANSWER: Tempura

ANSWER: Shovel

ANSWER: Monkey bars

ANSWER: A computer keyboard

I am filled with words. I come in every language, and I am really helpful. Yet, people still appreciate the internet more because that is where they look things up now. I contain the meaning of every word you can think of. It may be hard to use me, but the right definition is always hidden in my pages. What am I?

I can be a physical activity or I can be on a board. You can do this at home, outside, in school, on the computer, even on a piece of paper. I can be educational or just for fun. I am usually recommended for ages three and up, but not always. I help you spend quality time with your family. What am I?

I am small with little round edges around the top of me. I am the head of something you drink out of. People have collections of me from many years ago. I am made in factories around the world. Snapple has facts on the inside of me. Sometimes I am made out of plastic and sometimes metal. What am I?

I am a shelter for a part of your body. You can find me at malls or many stores. I usually have tracks on the bottom of me and holes for strings on the top. I can be used as a fashion statement or for comfort. What am I?

ANSWER: Dictionary

ANSWER: Games

ANSWER: Bottle cap

ANSWER: Shoes

VROOM! I suck-up all the dust, all the dirt, and even things I'm not supposed to. I could be very expensive, or I can be lousy and cheap. I may be small or can be big. I could be on low or on high. It all matters which way you set me. What am I?

I have a long neck and sometimes my legs are long, too. I am a gold colored animal with black spots all over my body. My main sources of food are leaves and buds from trees and shrubs. I am known for being very tall. What am I?

I am used to clean something. Once you turn me on, water sprouts out of me and sprays. I am mostly in a bathroom. On a beach, you will most likely find me outside. The first type of me was invented in the early 19th century. In some countries, I might be outside all the time. What am I?

I live in the ocean. I am a living thing. I am black and some grey. People eat me as an appetizer, usually raw. Some people like putting lemon on me when they eat me. I am usually closed shut until forced to open. You need a knife to open me. I sometimes produce pearls. What am I?

ANSWER: Vacuum

ANSWER: Giraffe

ANSWER: Shower

ANSWER: Oyster

I can be beautiful and I come in a lot of different colors. I can be in glue. Some people adore me and some people can't stand me. I can spill and make a big mess and it can be a huge pain to clean me up. I can be on clothes and in art. What am I?

I have four legs and a snout. Not many people keep me inside. There are races that involve me. When I am fully grown up, I am 4 ½ feet tall to 6 feet tall. There are many shows and books with me in them. I can jump over hurdles and speed down paths. I can live with others of my species or by myself. I eat a lot of food and drink a lot of water. There are many places for me to stay all over the world. What am I?

I am with you most of the day. You could say that I know you really well. You sometimes get me dirty. Some people couldn't care less about me. Some people think of me every second of the day. I can be plain or colorful. I can be intricate or boring. I am something companies may get a lot of money for. There are some companies who have made loads of money, and have been successful. What am I?

Some people like to have me as their pet. I am a flying animal. I can be bright and vibrant or plain and dull. There are hundreds of different species of me. My scientific name is Aves. People think I am the last living example of dinosaurs. Hundreds of species of me are threatened because of mankind. What am I?

ANSWER: Glitter

ANSWER: Horse

ANSWER: Clothes

ANSWER: Bird

The color of me is unique. There are many different ways to make me, but there are a few ingredients you need to make me. A clown invented me by accident, involving candies. I can be ordered in restaurants or can be bought. I am mostly water, but that is not all. I was invented in Chicago. Some people sweeten me with honey or sugar. An ingredient you need to make me is an ingredient that you probably don't want to eat by itself. What am I?

I sit in utter silence and wait for someone to pick me up and look at me. Beep, someone taps on me and unlocks me. There are different brands that make me that have different features. Some people go overboard on me, and some people don't care that much about me. I am a source of communication. I have a built-in camera. What am I?

I love to get my belly rubbed. I love to get a delicious treat when I'm obedient. I can be trained to sit, roll over, or even guide a blind person. My scientific name is Canis lupus familiaris. There are a lot of different types of me. People might be allergic to me. My enemy starts with c, but sometimes I become friends with that enemy. Some people say that I am man's best friend. What am I?

I'm used at the Olympics. I am a piece of equipment for a sport. I can also be a sort of art. When you are on me you have to balance so you don't fall off. You can do many tricks on me like jumping and leaping. Just make sure you don't fall off! I am long and thin. What am I?

ANSWER: Pink lemonade

ANSWER: Phone

ANSWER: Dog

ANSWER: Balance beam

I'm one of the largest and strongest predators in the world. There are many types of me. I swim around the sea, looking for prey to devour. Most people and animals fear me, so nobody really likes me. My eyes are on different sides of my face. My teeth are really big, which is a reason why most animals are afraid of me. My great sense of smell can sense blood more than a mile away. What am I?

I am a currency that is not printed. I am mined, but not physically. I am the first of my kind. My value is always changing. My creator is Satoshi Nakamoto. It is quite hard to understand how I work, because I am a stock. I am electronic and people use me to buy things. What am I?

I follow you around wherever you go. I can be seen during certain times of the day. You can't get away from one of me, especially when the sun is out. I am going to be with you for your entire life. What am I?

I'm a very solid object with different pieces. I am used for protecting a part of the human body while a person plays a sport. If they don't wear me in this sport, they would probably get very injured. I used to be made out of leather in the early 1900's to the mid 1950's. I am now made out of plastic. What am I?

ANSWER: Shark

ANSWER: Bitcoin

ANSWER: Shadow

ANSWER: Football helmet

Some toddlers play many different games with me. There are numerous types of me. I can be big or small. People use me in different ways. I can be one or multiple colors. The most common way is to throw me into the air. I am used in many sports. What am I?

I'm made of a few materials, but am hard to make. I go on a certain part on your face. I help people with one of their senses. There are many different types of lenses used for me. What am I?

Some people love me. Others don't ever want to pick me up. I can be small or big in size, but usually no bigger than a school desk. I can have pictures. There are many types of me. There are people that create me and hope to make money off of me. I can be good or bad. There is a long process in making me. What am I?

You need me for making purchases. Some people feel better when they have more of me. I'm green and only stare at you when you're looking at my face. Another form of me could be round and silver in color, although these aren't worth as much as my green cousins. If you didn't have me then life could be harder. What am I?

ANSWER: Ball

ANSWER: Glasses

ANSWER: Books

ANSWER: Money

I am known as a slow-poke. I'm actually the slowest animal in the world. My scientific name is 'Folivora.' I spend my days mostly in the trees or sleeping. My kind rarely climbs down from the trees and can live for up to 30 years. I like to sleep by hanging by my claws from tree branches. I live in Central and South America, enjoying the tall trees found in rainforests. What am I?

If it's raining, you use me. If there is a thunderstorm, I am not too useful. In movies, I can be seen inside out. I can go from big to small very quickly. I have a metal structure, but the covering keeps you dry and warm. If I'm opened inside your house, I am considered bad luck. What am I?

I have a bumpy texture. You will notice that I am usually orange, but you can get me in a few different colors. I am round and I am either passed, thrown, or dribbled in a game. I am used in many different practice drills and when I am handled too much by kids (especially outside), I get a little discolored. What am I?

I am one giant tangle within minutes of cooking me. I am usually boiled. I'm from Italy, but most people in the world know of me. I'm eaten with or without sauce. Sometimes chefs put a little bit of basil on me. What am I?

ANSWER: Sloth

ANSWER: Umbrella

ANSWER: Basketball

ANSWER: Spaghetti

I come in many different variations. I can be sparkly, stretchy, gooey, tough, jiggly, etc. I can shaped in whatever way you choose. I can be made with many different ingredients like shaving cream, but you can put other things in me for a different consistency. Some people like to give me color. I am/was a trendy item to make that is all over the internet. What am I?

I'm not really liked. If I'm doubled, you'll probably hear a groan from everyone. Sometimes people forget me and some people remember me all the time. I am usually on paper, but I could be on a computer, too. I might require you to do experiments or do something physical. Once you're done with me a lot of people are happy, but teachers will give more of me the next day anyway. What am I?

I'm all around you. If I wasn't there for a long time, then you would be gone. I'm invisible, but I'm always there. I see you do your homework, play with your friends and watch a movie with your family. Trees help provide me outside. What am I?

Though I am a very lovable animal, most people love another animal more than me. There are constant debates on which is better. I land on my feet every time I fall. Legend says that I have nine lives. I have a powerful sense of smell, and a powerful sense of sight. There are over 200 breeds of me! What am I?

ANSWER: Slime

ANSWER: Homework

ANSWER: Oxygen

ANSWER: Cat

People think I'm cute and some don't. I am a carnivore. I have the same color fur as a fox and the same type of fur like a dog. I communicate by barking or howling to get my friends' attention. What am I?

I am known for my spots. I am a small insect. Some people think we are bugs, but we are actually beetles. Part of my name refers to the Virgin Mary. My bright colors warn predators to stay away. I am one of the best loved insects. What am I?

I stand up tall, sometimes on a pole. My colors are very well known - red, white, and blue. Every day people pledge to me. I wave myself through the wind. I have stars and stripes on me. What am I?

I am a pink animal. I have a snout. I am a farm animal. Almost every farm has me. My main hobby is to roll around in the mud. Some people eat me for breakfast, lunch, and dinner, but I do not like that. What am I?

ANSWER: Dingo

ANSWER: Ladybug

ANSWER: American flag

ANSWER: Pig

The more I was moved and touched the less my master would enjoy me. I heard the doorbell and muffled voices. I knew the children had come to take me away and put me in their buckets. I knew that I would be taken away from my candy friends and eaten. What am I?

Most of you despise me. I just mean to help you get better. I range from hundreds of different colors, starting from kelly green to pale white. You leave me in a lonely corner with no friends. Your parents may buy me, but you won't touch me unless you are smart and want to get stronger. Your parents may sneak me in so you don't know, but when I am in plain sight you may not like me. What am I?

I either have a hard shell or a soft shell. I can have all sorts of meat in me, or have vegetables, or both. I usually have many toppings. A lot people like to eat me for lunch and dinner. People use me in a phrase, and like to eat me on Tuesday. People like to have chips with me. People sometimes have more than one of me. I am a Mexican dish. What am I?

I was considered a planet in 1930, until the year 2006, when scientists considered me a dwarf planet. I was the ninth planet, but now I'm not even a planet. I start with the letter P, and I am named after a Disney character. Well actually a dog so…. What am I?

ANSWER: Halloween candy

ANSWER: Vegetables

ANSWER: Taco

ANSWER: Pluto

My bright colors may deceive you, but don't be fooled by my beauty. I'm very dangerous and can be and very hard to spot. In ancient times I was used as poison for arrows. The darts of my poison are fatal, used by natives in the land of Rain. I can be orange, green, and yellow. Also, the brighter I am, the more dangerous and deadly I am. What am I?

I am black striped and orange, covered with a white belly. I love to climb trees and hang out around shade. I live in mostly northern India and China. I am also found in Austria. I am an endangered animal, and I am a carnivore. My scientific name is Panthera tigris. What am I?

I am a flaming ball of fury. I'm the basis of all life. I give off radiant light. I am mostly drawn yellow in kids' pictures, but I am actually all the colors mixed together. I can burn out with a gigantic explosion. I am 92.96 million miles away from our planet. What am I?

I am filled with a lot of words. I can be online or in a book. Some people think I am boring, but I'm actually pretty useful if you think about it. The most obvious reason you use me is because you don't what a word means or don't understand. What am I?

ANSWER: Poison dart frog

ANSWER: Tiger

ANSWER: Sun

ANSWER: Dictionary

Some people would rather use me instead of typing on a computer. I can be used for multiple reasons. Some people chew on me when they are nervous, like on tests. There are two types of me. For one type of me, you use a device to make me sharp. For the other type, you don't need the device, but you could run out of the thing to make me work. What am I?

I can dig a hole to hide my body in five minutes. My body might be a little fat, but I can defend myself from a hyena. My nose is long, but my tongue is longer. I look like an anteater. I am a nocturnal mammal. If you write a group of animals in alphabetical order then I will probably be in the front. What am I?

I am very good, and I come in over 100 varieties. I am usually all different colors and flavors, such as chocolate or strawberry. I can be filled, covered in a glaze, or just plain. You can buy me in grocery stores, or places that are dedicated to selling me. What am I?

In the early 1900s, I was the biggest ship in the world. My maiden voyage went from England to New York. I was in the middle of my journey when I hit an iceberg. I filled up with water and sank to the bottom of the Atlantic Ocean. When I sank, I split in two and more than half of my passengers died at sea. I am remembered as a tragic event in history. What am I?

ANSWER: Pencil

ANSWER: Aardvark

ANSWER: Donut

ANSWER: The Titanic

I am a flying insect with large, fragile wings. My life cycle goes from egg to larva to pupa, then finally, adult. I have six legs. My job is to fly to certain places like flowers to pollinate them, grass, or even somewhere around your house. I am half an inch to around a foot in size. What am I?

I am bigger than my other neighbors, but am pretty small compared to some of my other ones. My body is made of gas. My closest friend lives a few million miles away. I have rings around me, but they are super thin. You definitely know one of my friends. In fact, you are probably on it right now. Without it, you would die. I am a Roman god's name, but my Greek name is Poseidon. What am I?

When I no longer can be with you, you will replace me. Most people have me. You probably have different kinds of me, for different times of the year. There are other colors and sizes of me. I keep your feet warm and safe from sharp objects. What am I?

You can find me around the bottom of the ocean. I like to cling onto things. I have more legs and eyes than you, most likely. But don't worry because I won't harm you. I am not usually the first thing that pops in your head when you think of animals in the ocean. I am a character in the T.V. show *Spongebob Squarepants*. What am I?

ANSWER: Butterfly

ANSWER: Neptune

ANSWER: Shoes

ANSWER: Starfish

I am usually a cylinder shape that closes off into a cone at the top. You can store any liquid in me. I am very useful to have when at a sports game. I'm usually blue or clear. There are a lot of brands that make me, like Poland Springs or Dasani. What am I?

I was one of the best selling products of 2007. A lot of people own one of me and a lot of people are addicted to me, but other people prefer different companies over me. I have cool features, like a flashlight, compass, calculator, etc. I was made by Steve Jobs and many other inventors. You can take pictures with me. What am I?

If you leave crumbs from your snack, I clean it up for you. I am used on all kinds of hard floors, but usually not carpet. There is a plant that has the same name as me. The person who invented me was Levi Dickenson. There is a tool that might come with me that helps you collect the things I clean. In fairy tales, witches like to ride me in the sky. What am I?

Other people use me more than you do. People probably mention it every day to you. There are a lot of me and I can be in any language. Your mom and dad probably have chosen which one of me would be best for you. You might change me later. Every person probably has me. What am I?

ANSWER: Water bottle

ANSWER: iPhone

ANSWER: Broom

ANSWER: Your Name

I am common for traveling to really faraway places. Some people like to go on me and some people don't like to because they get sick or nervous. I have people who operate me and drive me. You might think it is one time when you are on me, but when you get to where you are going, it's sometimes a different time. Some of me are more expensive than others. The Wright brothers invented the first type of me. What am I?

I fly through the air like a bird. I spin in the air. When I start to fall in your hands, you try to catch me. If you can't catch me, I hit the ground. I am sold all over the world. I am stiff and covered in leather. I used to be made out of natural materials like pig bladder. My weight is usually 410-450 grams. What am I?

I can be in any subject in school. Depending on your life, you might have me outside of school, too. Nobody really likes me. In school, once you get into higher grades, you will be getting more of me. There is most likely some of me in every school over the world. I can be on the computer, or on paper, or require you do an experiment and much more. What am I?

I am round. I come in many designs but my most well known design is just black and white. I am called something different in North America than the other parts of the world. People kick me. They sometimes hit me with their heads. What am I?

ANSWER: Airplane

ANSWER: Football

ANSWER: Test

ANSWER: Soccer ball

I've seen the ins and outs of your house. I'm watching you and you don't know it. If you need me I'm there for you. Food, dirt, and dust - I eat it all. Every once in awhile I eat other things that I shouldn't. There are hundreds of different types of me. I can be cheap or I can be expensive. What am I?

I grow on trees in tropical locations. I am white on the inside and I have husk on the outside. People come up in the trees to get me and they shave the insides out of me. I can be very hard to open. Sometimes they put me in ice cream, drinks, and even your breakfast. What am I?

I am a fierce predator that strives to be independent. My kind always tries to be better than each other. I can run up to 40 miles per hour. I use my speed to chase down animals. My two primary fur colors are orange and black. What am I?

I am a gift from France. I am a worldwide famous landmark. My color changed over the years from a copper color, to a murky greenish blue. I have many symbols that are related to the United States of America, such as having thirteen spikes that resemble the thirteen colonies. I represent Libertas, a Greek goddess. What am I?

ANSWER: Vacuum

ANSWER: Coconut

ANSWER: Tiger

ANSWER: The Statue of Liberty

I am used to represent a famous day in the U.S. I usually take place at night, as that's the best time to see me. I can be used in other countries, too, but for different reasons. I have many different colors and I can look sparkly. Every time I work, I normally make a loud noise. What am I?

Standing tall and strong I bet I have scared some kids. They probably think I am going to fall. I love the crowds of people that swarm me. I live in Italy and one of my favorite things to do is lean. What am I?

I am on your face. Some people say there is disgusting stuff inside me. I can tell if food smells good or bad. If you don't have me you will not be able to breathe properly. I like to sniff and check if something is fishy. Some girls like to put ornaments on me. If I am good you will look sharp. If you don't have me, you most likely can't smell things. What am I?

I am green. I am a great partner for tortilla chips. I was first created by the Aztecs in what is now Mexico. I'm a delicious dip, and one of the most known Mexican dips in the world. The name is derived from two Aztec Nahuatl words - ahuacatl and molli. I am made with avocados and some other ingredients. What am I?

ANSWER: Fireworks

ANSWER: Leaning Tower of Pisa

ANSWER: Nose

ANSWER: Guacamole

I am filled with goodness. You can make me many ways. I can be full of vegetables, meat, or whatever you want. I hold the filling with a soft floury bread, which is usually creamy white. Some people don't like the bread, but most do. I am a Mexican food. What am I?

Sometimes people lose me. Some schools or public libraries have me for people to use. I sometimes can be anywhere, including classrooms. You could buy me or make me yourself. You use me to save your spot in a book. What am I?

I am a food. I used to be a vegetable, grain, and a fruit. I am usually a white to orange color. I can be served with butter, salt, chocolate, or other delicious ingredients. Native Americans discovered me. You can microwave me, kettle cook me, or cook me on a stove. You also can find quite a bit of me at movie theaters. What am I?

A lot of people like to draw on me, color on me, and sometimes scribble on me. Sometimes people rip me up into pieces. I can be used for homework, to make books, magazines, and many other things. Part of me comes from trees. What am I?

ANSWER: Burrito

ANSWER: Bookmark

ANSWER: Popcorn

ANSWER: Paper

There are different types of me. You can eat me for a snack with a dip, or just eat me plain. There are many brands that make me so I have a variety of looks. My common colors are yellow and orange. I usually make a crunchy sound when you eat me. What am I?

I am an animal that's been around on earth for a long time. I can be deadly, especially if you bother me. Many people run away from me. In America I live in coastal areas with a tropical climate or swampy waters. I have scaly skin. When cooked, people say I taste like chicken. What am I?

I am known as a delicacy on the shore and coast. I am a ferocious creature of the deep and a dream to all fishermen. I am a monster to catch and big in commercial fishing. I can be around 10 feet long in length when fully grown. I am also known as the Bonito shark in some areas. Fishermen would be delighted to have my jaw on their wall. What am I?

I am flat and dry. I was born in the southeast of Europe. Another name for me is the flap jack. There are different types of me such as the korean, chinese, mung beans, and others. I go very well with butter and syrup. I am also known as breakfast. What am I?

ANSWER: Chips

ANSWER: Alligator

ANSWER: Mako shark

ANSWER: Pancakes

I can help you lose weight. I also build muscle. I have vitamins C, E, B1, B3, B5, and B6. There are many brands that sell me, but naturally I am the best, especially when you drink me out of my shell. My shell can be hard to open, but once opened just stick a straw in me and I am yours. What am I?

I am a type of food. I can be plain or I can have many kinds of toppings. One of my more popular toppings is pepperoni, but you could have me with pineapple, bacon, or even anchovies. I am a good food for parties. I was created in June 1889. There are a lot of restaurants that are famous for me. October is my national month. What am I?

ANSWER: Coconut milk

ANSWER: Pizza

www.ingramcontent.com/pod-product-compliance
Lightning Source LLC
Chambersburg PA
CBHW071526040426
42452CB00008B/905